JANUARY 2022

AN ANTHOLOGY OF ARTICLES

BRAIN BOOSTER ARTICLES

Contents

Contents

Preface

"Start writing, no matter what. The water does not flow until the faucet is turned on".

-Louis L'Amour

This book is a bouquet of articles contributed by students, professors and academicians. Hundreds of students and professors are contributing their work to Brain Booster Articles, we are here to provide ample information about Law and Contemporary issues. Our aim is to provide a platform for today's generation to express their views and ideas on law and contemporary law.

CHAPTER ONE

HOW DATA PROTECTION BILL IS ANTICIPATED TO IMPACT THE WAY PEOPLE THINK ABOUT AND PRACTICE PRIVACY?

Author: Harshita Tholiya, II year of B.A.,LL.B.(Hons.) from University Five Year Law College, University Of Rajasthan, Jaipur

Harshita Tholiya

If you want to question the government or get some information from them. You can take advantage of RTI Act, 2005. If a person wants to prevent superfluous intervention, he can utilise his right to privacy, which he has against the government, journalists, and even neighbours. A UN report on the road map for digital cooperation 2020 presented that more than 7000 data breaches were recorded in 2019 exposing more than 15 billion records. The potential cost of worldwide data breaches will be more than 5 trillion by 2024.1

"Data is the oil of the 21st century."

-Clive Humbly

With the widespread use of computers and the internet on a global scale. Data is collected, and surfing patterns and online behaviour of users are tracked in order to serve adverts to targeted people in order for businesses to profit. A lot of data is saved online without the user's agreement, and the corporation bears no duty or liability for the data leakage.

Individuals' data privacy must be protected, which necessitates legislation that lays out procedures for handling data appropriately. Procedures for using, collecting, storing, and sharing personal data must be clearly mentioned. Furthermore, the legislation must recognize the right to reasonable control over personal data. And strict adherence to such laws must be ensured.

<u>What Is Data Privacy?</u>

Data privacy refers to the proper treatment of data in accordance with established rules, such as the General Data Protection Regulation (GDPR) drafted by the European Union in 2018 or the GDPR-compliant laws enacted by the country. Data privacy concerns the collection, storage, management, and sharing of data, as well as compliance with current privacy regulations.2

<u>Data Protection In India History</u>

The (Indian) Information Technology Act, 2000 addresses concerns such as civil compensation and criminal penalties for improper disclosure and misuse of personal data, as well as breaches of contractual agreements relating to personal data.

A body corporate that is in possession, dealing, or handling any sensitive personal data or information, and is negligent in implementing and maintaining reasonable security practises, resulting in wrongful loss or wrongful gain to any person, may be held liable to pay damages to the person so affected under section 43A of the (Indian) Information Technology Act, 2000. The 2011 Rules on Information Technology (Reasonable Security Practices and Procedures and Sensitive Personal Data or Information). Only "Sensitive personal data" is protected under the Rules.3

Present scenario

Recently, the Parliamentary panel also known as Joint Parliamentary Committee headed by BJP MP PP Chaudhary adopted the final draft of the Data Protection Bill which was originally drafted in 2018 by Justice B.N. Srikrishna and consists of 98 clauses.4

Key Terms

1. Data Principal: The person whose data is being talked about i.e. stored, collected or processed is called data principal.
2. Data Fiduciary: Data fiduciary refers to the entity or person who decides on the means and purposes of data processing.
3. Data processing: The Bill regulates how the government and corporations established in India process personal data.
4. Data localization: It applies to foreign companies dealing with the personal data of Indian citizens. It means storing sensitive data in India only.
5. General consent: The bill gives the data subject significant rights over their personal information. Any processing of personal data can only take place with the consent of the data subject.
6. Data Protection Authority: The Bill establishes a DPA to ensure compliance with Bill's requirements and to provide for additional restrictions regarding the handling of personal data of individuals.5

The bill specifies the following types of data

The data is a valuable asset to the nation. And if it is categorised properly and protected accordingly could reduce the risk of data breaches, cyber-attacks, fake news and could even polish up the tax regime.

1. Personal data

It refers to information such as a person's name, address, and other identifying characteristics that can be stored and processed in or outside of India

2. Sensitive Personal Data

This is the individual's sensitive data, such as gender, health, financial status, caste, and so on. In India, this data could be stored and processed. To process data outside of the nation, the Data Protection Authority must provide permission.

3. Critical Personal Data

This category deals with sensitive information pertaining to the military, defence, and national security. This information is exclusively saved and processed in India.

4. Non-Personal Data

This is information that is not personally identifiable. For instance, traffic patterns, demography, and so forth. It is collected by the government for the benefit of people which includes schemes and subsidies. And the government is not required to take any consent of people to collect data from the fiduciary.6

Provisions Of Data Protection Bill, 2019

If data falls into the wrong hands, it may be used to disseminate fake news, hate speech, and even influence elections. Prior to this statute, data security has not kept pace with advancements in hacking and espionage. To resolve these issues, the Data Protection Bill, 2019 was drafted.

Its goal is to protect people's privacy when it comes to their personal information i.e. giving access to their Right to Privacy which was established explicitly in K.S. Puttaswamy v.s. Union Of India7 is also known as Aadhaar Act. In this case, National Identity was accused of infringing on a person's right to privacy. In the case of M.P. Sharma v. Satish Chandra8, the Advocate General of India endorsed the Indian government's contention that Indian people do not enjoy such rights guaranteed in the Indian Constitution. A nine-judge panel unanimously declared in August 2017 that Indians have a right to privacy. There is also no requirement for a separate declaration. This right is adequately protected by Articles 14, 19, and 21.

Nine principles of data privacy include consent, notice, correction, purpose, removal of data etc. This bill also aims to define the flow and use of personal data, as well as to establish a bond of trust between entities and individuals processing personal data. Individuals whose personal data is processed will also have their rights protected under the bill. It will also establish a framework for data processing organisational and technical measures.

It will lay down norms for

1. Social media intermediary: To prevent anonymity, social media intermediaries such as telecom, network, internet, and site hosting service providers are required to conduct thorough verification. To assure the operability of its Indian branches, the parent business must open an office in India. Data stored and collected must be justified and commensurate to the purpose for which it is taken.9

2. Accountability of entities processing personal data: The main goal is purpose limitation and collection limitation, i.e. storing and processing personal data for only justifiable or legal purposes with the user's knowledge and consent

But in cases of

i)medical emergency

ii)legal proceedings i.e. investigation, detection and prevention of offences for the violence of laws.

iii)Government providing services or benefits to the individual, the consent is not required.10

3. Data transfer across borders: Personal data can be saved and processed everywhere, however sensitive personal data can only be stored and processed with the consent of the Data Protection Authority.

4. Remedies for unauthorised and harmful processing:

(i) processing or transferring personal data in violation of the Bill, which is punishable by a fine of Rs 15 crore or 4% of the fiduciary's annual turnover, whichever is higher, and

(ii) inability to conduct a data audit, which is punishable by a fine of Rs 5 crore or 2% of the fiduciary's annual turnover, whichever is higher. Without consent, re-identification and processing of de-identified personal data are punishable by up to three years in prison, a fine, or both.11

5. Establish an Indian Data Protection Authority: An Indian Data Protection Authority must be established, and each organisation must employ Data Protection Officers to ensure that the regulations are followed.

6. Right to be forgotten: This law is in congruence with the guidelines set by General Data Protection Regulations by the European Union. It limits the further disclosure of their personal information by fiduciary if it does not serve any purpose or the consent is revoked.

What are the concerns regarding this bill?

1. Exemptions: Clause 35 of the proposed data protection bill, which has sparked controversy, allows the government and its agencies to get

blanket exemptions from all of the bill's provisions, with no checks and balances in place. The Aadhaar Authority, UIDAI, and the Income Tax Department already have exemptions from the bill. Proper judicial oversight must be done and a more detailed prescription for agencies that can access data and when.

2. The hegemony of the executive branch: The executive's decision to issue such an order is not subject to oversight.

3. Unprecedented and intrusive: The current rules for protecting civilians from arbitrary and intrusive government surveillance, as revealed by the Pegasus case, are ineffective. The action was taken by the government.12

4. Question Of Reasonability: Government can use data for reasonable causes but this reasonability is arbitrary and not clearly mentioned.

5. Encryption Of Data: The level of data encryption determines the vulnerability to cyber-attacks. However, there are no specific provisions in this bill that address it.

6. Protective Policy: If data is exclusively saved in India, MNCs with servers in other countries that keep their users' data may experience challenges, which could stymie economic policy.

7. Start-ups: Due to the limits established to protect data, Indian startups operating abroad may risk reprisal. It will make conducting business more challenging.

8. Lack of User Awareness: Users are unaware of technical concepts such as cookies, required permissions, and the ramifications of granting such permissions.

9. Data Localisation: Any other state, or any other anti-social institution, could be able to monitor user data.13

Best practises are used all throughout the world

The General Data Protection Regulation (GDPR) in Europe is often regarded as the apex of data protection regulation worldwide. A separate statute dealing with the processing of personal data by law enforcement agencies is in existence under EU law. Part 3 of the UK's Data Protection Act liberalises certain requirements while simultaneously guaranteeing that data protection rights are protected.14

A Way forward

It's strenuous to strike a balance between privacy concerns and public demands (such as national security). This should go through extensive consultations in Parliament, with all interests represented. One can only hope that once considered in Parliament, sufficient time and attention is given to establishing a better balance between opposing interests.

The need of the hour is to establish clear and comprehensive laws and ensure their implementation at the earliest. Meanwhile, other companies must take proactive steps to protect the privacy of the users. And more awareness and empowerment should be given to consumers.

CHAPTER TWO

SHOULD MARITAL RAPE BE CRIMINILSED UNDER SECTION 377?

Author: Mohammad Azhad Hasan, Pursuing B.B.A.,LL.B. from The NorthCap University

Recently many petitions are filed in Delhi High court to criminalize marital rape under Section 377 by various women organizations in the effect of increased marital rape.

According to National Crime Record Bureau (NCRB) in India, 70% of women are the victim of domestic violence, in recent times marital rape is now one of its kind. According to World Bank data more than 100 countries have criminalized marital rape but India is part of 36 countries that is yet to criminalize marital rape.

In recent Chhattisgarh, high absolved a man from facing a trial allegedly raping wife on the pretext that Indian law does not recognize marital rape if the wife is above 15 years of age. Justice N.K Chandravanshi on hearing the case relied upon the exception of Section 375 which says that "sexual intercourse or sexual act by a man with his wife, the wife not being under fifteen years of age, is not rape ". This judgement draws criticism from various segments of the society especially from women organizations because women have been treated still as property of the husband.

Before the enactment of the Indian Penal Code 1860, rape was not a crime against women, as they are considered property of father before marriage and after marriage, their husband, any crime against women is considered to be done against their father and husband and they are the one-take action. After the enactment of IPC 1860, the crime against women was considered to be against them and they have all right to take action, but the offence of rape was limited to sexual intercourse without the consent of the woman and did not recognize marital rape.

HISTORY

In Babylonia 1900 BCE, a man would be punishable by death if he had sexual intercourse with another man wife or daughter, considering the woman is property of his father or husband. Rape was considered a property crime in the ancient period due which husband raping a wife or father raping his daughter is not considered a crime. In the 18th and 19th-century rape laws were introduced by British Empire because rape violates the sexual purity of women and any husband would not violate his wife sexual purity and hence again with another theory rape by husband is not a crime. Due to this conservative mindset Doctrine of Coverture become legal doctrine in common law whereby, upon marriage, a woman`s legal rights and obligations were subsumed by those of her husband. Due to these crimes, there was a sense of need to draft the Indian Penal Code.

Section 375 of IPC 1860 recognize rape as a crime against women and cover various type of rapes such as gang rape, campus rape etc. but did not recognize marital rape. Under Exception 2 of the given section, it is not raped if the husband forces her wife until she is less than 15 years of age. To criminalize marital rape Exception two has to be deleted.

WHAT ARE PROBABLE ARGUMENTS THAT WILL SATISFY TO CRIMINALIZE MARITAL RAPE

One of the main arguments is that even in the 21st-century women are treated as the property of the husband even though they have their rights and obligations which are protected by the supreme authority that is the constitution of India. Also, Exception 2 of Section 375 violates Article 14 by differentiating married women from unmarried. Another argument is that this act only held the husband liable when the girl is less than 15 years of age whereas the Prevention of Children from Sexual Offences Act (POCSO Act) recognize crime against women in the minor category till the age of 18 years. After the 2013 constitution amendment, the legal age for consent under section 375 has been increased from 15 to 18 but Exception 2 of the same section consider crime only when the woman is less than 15 years of age. Sexual intercourse with the wife without her consent infringes the right to autonomy given in Article 21.

ARGUMENTS AGAINST CRIMINALIZING MARITAL RAPE

Marriage is legal and formally recognized union of two people, both are associated partners who are together with mutual consent, as marriage is considered to be a legal contract between the parties in association there exist implied consent which gives both a right to indulge in sexual intercourse, so we can say that there exists a consent which is implied. Section 498a recognize crime against married women by her husband and relatives which partially cover marital rape by recognizing the act done without her consent. One of the main arguments is that there are increased cases of harassment against men by falsely implicating them under the Domestic Violence Act and marital rape is criminalized then there will be more cases where men are put behind bars by false implication.

<u>CONCLUSION</u>

Looking at present times it is difficult to determine whether marital rape should be criminalized or not because it is difficult for the parliament to strike the balance between various stereotypical approaches which governs society and its association.

CHAPTER THREE

WAS THE DECISION TO INCREASE LEGAL AGE OF MARRIAGE FOR GIRLS IS RIGHT?

<u>**Author**</u>: Saima Hasan, I year of B.B.A.,LL.B. from North Cap University

Recently, the Cabinet has passed a proposal to increase the minimum age of marriage for women from 18 to 21 years old, claiming that it would empower women and will help to eradicate child marriage.

In June 2020, Ministry of Women and Child Development setup a task force which was headed by Jaya Jaitly, talking to TOI she said the reason to increase women age of marriage is not to control population because it is already controlled. According to latest data mortality rate of India is 2.0 which perfectly under control, the real agenda behind is to improve women reproductive health after marriage,motherhood related problem like maternal mortality rate and death of mother after childbirth. To reduce age for marriage this task force took feedback from 16 universities and various other NGO`s. But here the real issue is to control child marriage which in turn increases the rate of motherhood problems.

<u>WHAT IS CHILD MARRIAGE PROBLEM?</u>

According to 2019 estimates, more than 1.5 million girls in Indian weren`t 18 years old at the time of their marriage. If we look global number of child brides, one-third are from India, but the most shocking fact is that, according to NFHS 2019-20201 data 23% marriages are child marriages. Does that mean one-fifth of the people are violating the law? To understand we need to understand history of child marriages.

About 100 years ago, in 1917 some women came together to establish the Women's Indian Association. An association to raise the issue related to women, in front of then British Empire. But unfortunately , theBritishers were not interested in bringing these social reforms , so they approached India Freedom Fighters like Motilal Nehru and Mahatma Gandhi requesting them to raise these issues infront of British empire. In 1929 on Gandhi Ji advice Harbilas Sharda introduced a Bill, to restrain child marriages. Under this pressure British India Parliament passed Child Marriage Restraint Act,1929. According to this act, minimum marriage age for girls was fixed at 14 years and for boys it was fixed at 18 years. But actually implementing this law did not bring any benefits to the British, so they didn't really try to popularize this act and implementing at ground level that is why there is not much change. The next major step was taken after the Independence, in 1949 when the minimum marriage age for girls was raised from 14 to 15 years. And then in 1978, it was raised even further from 15 to 18 years old and in the same year, this age was raised for men from 18 to 21 years old. Under this act, the offences were no cognizable, before this, if you complained about a child marriage taking place then action could be taken based on your complaint, but now, he authorities could take action on their own even if no one complained about it.

But even after this, authorities were hardly concerned and the ground reality didn't change much. The most important change took place in the year 2006, The Prohibition of Child Marriage Act, 2006 this was the first time that child brides were given the option to have their marriage declared void. Before this, they had to go through divorce once the child marriage had taken place. But now, if someone is victim of child marriage they could go and complain and their marriage would be cancelled. Section 3 of this act say that every child marriage is voidable, but,there was a time limit for this rule, the marriage can be declared void only till 2 years after attaining the marriage age. Once the age limit is crossed the child marriage couldn't be cancelled after that, and this was a big loophole in the law. The things were so weird, that till 2017 the age of consent for physical relations was 18 years, but for a child bride, the same age was 15 years only. So we can say that, in a child marriage, marital rape was legal. Independent Thought, and NGO had filed a petition in the regarding this, thankfully our Supreme Court took an action regarding it and criminalized marital rape for girls below the age of 18. Theoretically, in Sections 9,10 and 11 of the 2006 Act, has the provisions of levying punishments, imprisonment for up to 2 years and fine up to rupees one lakh. But when the Act also contains that child marriage are voidable but cannot be automatically void then how would this law work. That`s why even today we can see, that 23% of all marriages are child marriages.

Hundreds of thousand of girls are married off at such a young age, but the cases registered regarding it is only a handful. Between 2014-2016, a mere 1785 cases were registered only and conviction was done only in 274 cases. This problem is not only found in India, many countries around the world have same problem. According to a 2010 UNFPA report, in 158 countries the legal age for marriage has been set at 18 years, but in 146 of these 158 countries the law allows the child marriage of girls with the consent of parents. Some countries have also taken positive action like Tanzania in Africa declared all marriages of children below the the age of 18 illegal.

WHAT ARE THE OBJECTIONS RAISED AFTER PROPOSAL IS PASSED?

The main objection was raised by Rajya Sabha MP Priyanka Chaturvedi, by sharing newspaper clip on Twitter showing the names daughters are given in some part of India like Dhapu(Feed Up), Ramghani(O`Ram it`s enough), and increasing there age for marriage will have more impact then child marriage. The main objection is that it is violating freedom of choice, because this act is restraining a 18 year old woman to choose when to marry and the same time she has a right to choose her MP,MLA. This act is also authoritative as it acting as guardian for the girl child restraining her freedom and treating her as property. This act also violates Article 14 which gives freedom to choose and Article 21 which gives right to personal liberty of the constitution.

ARGUMENTS IN FAVOUR

The decision by the central government because it is fundamentally against child marriages when the age limit is raised to 21 years, hopefully it will motivate people to have marriages at that age limit but at the same it should not be empty promise and with this child marriages should be declared illegal. The second argument is that this act will give time for girl child to be mentally and physically ready to marry. This act will also reduce motherhood problems and will also decrease malnutrition in children. The third argument was that this act will provide girl child to compete with male in education and carrier.

CONCLUSION

The increase in legal age for marriage is somewhat correct but only increasing the age will not do much. Infact, the task force on whose recommendation this Bill has been introduced has put forward more recommendations for bringing about societal change like increasing the accessibility for women in schools and colleges, easing transportation for women to schools and colleges and also focus on skill development and business training if these are also not implemented then this law will not be very effective. Government should also consider to completely ban child marriages. Central government "Beti Bachao, Beti Padhao" should not waste money just on advertisement but effectively implement it on ground level.

CHAPTER FOUR

BEYOND THE HORIZON OF IDENTIFICATION: ISSUE OF NON ACCEPTANCE OF LGBTQ WITH REFERENCE TO SOCIOLOGICAL THEORIES AND INDIAN LEGAL FRAMEWORK

Author: Iqra Siddiqui, LL.M.

Iqra Siddiqui

<u>ABSTRACT</u>

Gender identity and sexual orientation are the concepts which have been in controversy over a long time period. Sexual orientation reflects the sex of the person to whom one is attracted, sexually and romantically while the term Gender Identity describes an individual's inner sense of belonging to the male or the female gender category. This Article critically analyses the reasons pertaining to non acceptance of LGBTQ's sexual orientation in context of the Indian society with special reference to the Gender Socialization Theory, Functionalist Theory, and Labeling Theory of sociology. Further, the article claims that mere identification does not amount to acceptance. The claim is established by analyzing the shortcomings of the Indian legal framework. The law can pave a way for social inclusion of the marginalized LGBTQ community in the Indian society, if it is framed as per the need of the hour. The Indian Society is constantly evolving and the law must evolve with it, in order to redefine its nature and composition.

INTRODUCTION

Identification is the first step towards recognition. One of the major factors designated, to assign a person's identity, is the gender of that person. This determination is made at the birth of a child and accordingly a generalization of choices begins. The nursery is painted blue or pink leaving no option for a rainbow to spring.

Gender stereotyping is a frequently observed in all the dimensions of Indian society irrespective of culture, religion or origin. It has a keen association with the sexual orientation of an individual. The LGBTQ individuals become prey to this gender stereotyping of the society. A LGBTQ person's sexual orientation starts getting challenged, as soon as hormonal changes occur at the age of puberty. A state of complete dilemma leaves these teenagers in an unusual distress regarding their sexual orientation not falling in conformity with their identity.

HARMONIZING GENDER IDENTITY AND SEXUAL ORIENTATION

Gender Identity was coined as an expression in middle of 1960's as describing a person's inner sense of being a male of a female and henceforth belonging into the respective category.[1] This concept further evolved over time to involve those people who do not identify themselves in either of the aforementioned categories. Persons self perceived gender, irrespective of their biological sex, is Gender Identity.[2] Sexual orientation is a term relating to the sex of those individuals towards whom one is attracted, sexually and romantically.[3]

These concepts are severely misunderstood by the Indian society and hence the LGBTQ are treated as "the odd one out". Homosexuality is considered as a defect or disease and many a times people try getting it cured through medication, meditation or spiritual means. The issue begins with a person realizing a sense of belonging to the homosexual community and the challenge of accepting it as a reality. Homosexuals harmonize their gender identity with their sexual orientation diversifying themselves from the clutches of a heterosexual society.

SOCIOLOGICAL THEORIES ENCIRCLING HOMOSEXUALITY

GENDER SOCIALIZATION THEORY- This theory is based on the procedure or technique, males and females learn to be masculine or feminine through primary group interactions/ family and the way they are socialized into "traditional" gender roles.[4] Implying this theory, a newborn is treated either as a male or as a female child. As per the general practice, men are expected to display strength and courage in every situation whereas women should have traits like grace and beauty. This construct is implied on every individual and it becomes a guiding light of day to day conduct. This socialization occurs at every phase of life irrespective of the social agents one is surrounded by.

FUNCTIONALIST THEORY- Society is treated as an interrelated structure, like a social institution, with specific functions which are put together by applying consensus for letting the society function properly and to reproduce itself. [5] If any part of the society fails to work properly, the entire organism looks for a way to correct it so that the equilibrium is attained. [6]In simple words, if there is any behavior, conduct/ practice that is perceived to be interfering the social structure, society will look for a way applying shared norms and values, to discard it.

LABELLING THEORY- This theory is based on the idea, that behaviors become deviant only when society labels them so. The members of the society, who decipher certain conducts as deviant or bizarre, and then label individuals based on their understanding of deviance or non deviance. This theory focuses on, what labels are applied on whom and by whom, why are they applied and what is the consequence of such labeling.

<u>SIMILITUDE WITH INDIAN SOCIETY</u>

Family is considered to be the smallest unit of a society. The definition of family has changed from time to time but in generally the tradition and legal understanding of family is limited to married couples with children.[7] India adheres to this understanding, which becomes a major hindrance, in acceptance of LGBTQ's sexual orientation. Here, only a male and female are considered eligible to be a couple.

Since birth a person's gender is socialized and accordingly that person is expected to behave. If a man fails to show masculinity, he is shamed. If a woman does not display femininity, she is boycotted. The traits assigned to genders should be reflected in a person's behavior, to be included in the society. Those who fail to comply by these traits are considered as 'flawed'. Who does what, is based on a command, not a choice. Stereotypes like: Homosexual couples cannot be an eligible parent are entangled in the Indian society. If a person is perceived to be incapable of fulfilling a social role, then that person will be eliminated from the social structure, irrespective of that person's capability of fulfilling that role.

The major function of a family, in a society, as per the functionalist, is to reproduce and expand. The LGBTQ's relationships are discarded by the Indian society, basically because they cannot reproduce and hence does not lead to development. Neither they contribute to the stability nor do they maintain the social solidarity, in the society. Indian society being governed by religious laws, do not recognize marriages between same sex couples.

Homosexuals carry labels given by the society, of having low moral values, sexually incapable or psychologically incapable. They are considered deviant just because their sexual orientation is different from the mainstream. This impacts the life of homosexuals so drastically that, they generate a lower self esteem, leading to lack of confidence, affecting all arenas of their life.

<u>SHORTCOMINGS OF INDIAN LEGAL FRAMEWORK: A MAJOR FACTOR FOR NON ACCEPTANCE OF LGBTQ</u>

The fight for recognition was won by the LGBTQ, with the Partial decriminalization of section 377 I.P.C. This judgment removed one of the major difficulties, faced by homosexuals. Now, their identity is not criminalized; being a homosexual is now legal in India. But, is recognition, all that is needed, for a fulfilling life?

The transgender persons (protection of rights) Act, 2019, includes trans-men, trans-women, persons having inter sex variations, individuals having socio cultural identities and gender queers within the definition of transgender persons.[8] Though there is a lot of diversity within the homosexual community, still the act shadows it and portrays the entire community under a narrower term 'Transgender Persons'. The Act confers anti discriminatory rights and certain beneficial entitlements in areas of education, employment, health and welfare of transgender persons. It also provides for 'self perceived gender identities' yet it requires the transgender persons, to obtain a certificate of identity from the District Magistrate. The Act fails to make it clear, how transgender person will be treated under Indian civil and criminal laws, as they recognize only male and female gender.

"A marriage is solemnizes between a male and a transwomen, both professing Hindu religion, is a valid marriage in terms of section 5 of Hindu Marriage Act, 1955 and the Registrar of Marriage is bound to register the same." Arunkumar and Another v The Inspector general of registrar and Ors, WP (MD)No.4125 of 2019 and WMP(MD) No.3220 of 2019,Madras High Court (2019).

The court in this case, recognized a transwoman as a 'bride' under section 5 of Hindu Marriage Act, referring to self determination, individual autonomy and the freedom of self expression, summing up a transgender person's right to marry, the Madras High Court recognized it as the first case of transgender marriage in India.

The Matrimonial laws still do not include marriages between the homosexuals and are dependent on a legislation which could grant the homosexuals, Right to Marry ,as already declared by the Madras High Court, a right within article 21 of the Constitution. If this right is granted, by way of legislation, it will lead to break further barriers for the homosexuals which will eventually bring them out of the stigma attached to their existence.

Indian laws are prejudiced against homosexuals in terms of Adoption and Surrogacy Rights. They are deprived of the privilege, to have a family. They cannot adopt nor can they be surrogate parents. The Gender Socialization theory is so deep rooted in the Indian society that it diminishes the possibility of operating the functional theory for the homosexuals. In spite of the technological developments like surrogacy, homosexuals remain childless and despite of so many orphans being parentless, the homosexuals cannot adopt.

TO MOVE BEYOND THE HORIZONS: IMMIDATE REQUIREMENT OF AN EVOLVING SOCIETY

As a country, India is still under the tag of "developing" and "evolving" but the determination cannot be solely limited to the per capita income or standard of living. A country will actually show growth by breaking the bondages which weigh it down. The basic understanding of human rights, need to develop. The discriminatory mindset needs to evolve. If legislations grant the LGBTQ, basic rights like Marriage, Adoption and Surrogacy, this will be a great leap towards social inclusion of these marginalized groups.

Indian society has developed over time, through change, yet it is threatened, by change. It has accepted the diversity on cultural, linguistic and religious grounds, which is manmade, but is not ready to accept the diversity of Nature, in form of LGBTQ. The fear of breaking the social structure, which is also manmade, makes it unsusceptible to the idea of change. The country preaching "unity in diversity" fails to acknowledge a slight variation in its own kind.

Author's Biography

Iqra Siddiqui. She is a rhapsodist by desire, who loves to write about the social evils prevailing in the society. She pursued her LL.M from National Law University,Odisha and has a never-ending love for the poetic art of literature and law. She has an unconventional approach to living life to the fullest.A Future facilitator who is in a quest of making a better world for future generations through her legal sagacious outlook.

NATIONAL EDUCATIONAL POLICY, 2020 AND ITS IMPLEMENTATION IN THE TIMES OF COVID-19

Author: Gaurang Takkar, I year of B.A.,LL.B. from Army Institute of Law, Mohali

Gaurang Takkar

"An investment in knowledge pays the best interest"(1)
-Benjamin Franklin

Education is the building block of Comprehensive development of an Individual which entails the growth of Social, Economic, Political, Cultural and various other arenas of Human Intellect. There is a direct relationship between Education and National Emergence. Human Capital refers to the stock of Education , Health and Income of an individual etc and Investment in these areas directly result in country's development .

India's Education policy has a long history and if we talk about policies of Post-Independent era , there are 3 major educational policies which were introduced including the National Educational Policy , 2020.

NEP, 1968:- The first was introduced in 1968 and Kothari Commission was set up for that matter under the chairmanship of D.S. Kothari(2).It was entrusted with the task of dealing with all aspects and sectors of education and to advise the Government on the evolution of a National System of Education and as a result , NEP,1968 was formulated. Some of the highlights of this policy include:-

- Three Language Formula (which was highly criticized by people)
- Suggestion of Compulsory education for students of age 6 – 14
- Recommended 6% of GDP to be spent on Education

NEP, 1986:- The GOI initiated the National Policy on Education in 1986. Its ultimate objective was to provide education to all sections of society, with a particular stress on scheduled castes, scheduled tribes, other backward classes and women, who were deprived of educational opportunities for a long time. Some highlights of Policy include:-

- Focus on Primary Education
- Focus on establishment of open universities like IGNOU etc.
- Education to rural people
- Recommending a shift to Information Technology for cognitive development

NEP, 2020:- This is the most recent policy of GOI which was formulated under the chairmanship of K.Kasturirangan and was introduced in 2020 . Key highlights include :-

- Aim is to make India a "Global Knowledge Superpower"
- 100% Gross Enrolment Ratio in school education by 2030

- Universalisation of education
- Shift from old 10+2 system to a new system of 5+3+3+4
- Stress on MULTIDISCIPLINARY approach

This recent policy was to be implemented in 2020 itself but in the same year, The whole world was struck by a Pandemic which originated from Wuhan city of China which lies in Hubei province . It spread over the world in a very short span and India was definitely no exception. This led to a delay in implementation of this Policy which had strength to change the Indian education System almost entirely affecting Primary, Secondary and even Graduation level. It was a challenge to implement this Policy at the time of Online education but then also, This Policy started being implemented from session 2021-22 slowly and steadily. Karnataka became the first city to implement this New Education Policy.

Every Policy comes with its own sets of merits and demerits . This policy is a revolutionary one as it takes into consideration many of the problems which existed in earlier educational models and tried rectifying it. For example , the 3 language formula which was proposed earlier in 1968 policy and was highly criticised for having Hindi as a mandatory language , has now been changed to a more flexible one and is now left on state authority to decide what to be done in this regard. Earlier after class 10th , Students were bound to choose btw only 3 major streams for their secondary education which eventually left them with minimal career opportunities . But with NEP , 2020, Students are given a free hand on choosing their subject combination they are willing to study like Physics + Eco together OR Geography + Biology together etc. The concept of Vocational training is included in the curriculum whereby students will be experiencing internship like exposure from class 6th onwards through a 10-days No Bag schooling . Students will pay visits to nearby shops and markets or pharmacists where they will observe the professionals and get motivated. The Advantage of this will be the enhancement of social status of the people like carpenters , mechanics which as of now are seen with an eye of inferiority . There has also been a decision to increase spending of the government on Education to 6 % which is at present btw $3 - 4\%$.

Besides having many advantages , this policy has a handful of loopholes and pitfall. The policy has much broad and exaggerated targets . Some examples are - achieving a 100% Gross Enrolment Ratio(GER) By 2030 from 27.1% in 2019-2020 AND a jump from present 3-4% GDP spent on education to a spending of 6% . The reason for it being an over-expected target is that In 1968 policy itself , 6% was kept as a target expenditure which we are not able to achieve even in 2021. Other major limitation is regard to teaching students in Local lang till class 5th (Although its not made mandatory) but teaching for example in Hindi till 5th class and making a transition to English for Coding in 6th class can be a huge challenge and therefore the idea seems glim . This new policy provides many perks to SC,ST and OBC community but neglects the lower - Income General Category . The idea of teaching coding has its own set of problems . These include availability of skilled teachers which can make this subject an interesting one for students and Other is Affordability . Coding is a skill and any skill needs constant practice and diligence to show some results in that arena . Majority of people will not be in a position to afford for their children, a perfect coding setup which could hinder their education . In times of Covid-19, many people have lost their jobs and are earning very less. These expenditures can put them in lot of debt and financial problem. Already they have spent a lot on their online classes. Any more burden can cause counterproductive results.

This Policy is a very optimistic one and can be very beneficial for the country's overall development but needs certain altercations and solutions so that it can be made more useful and friendly and people can embrace it with open arms. One of the important thing that can be done is to announce this as a For-Profit System and not Not-For profit system. This will result in investments towards the educational sector of society and the expenditure will increase in this arena . Instead of teaching students in their local lang till class 5th, A Blend of language can be more helpful as English will not be an alien language for them when they enter in their Middle stage (6th-8th). Subsiding Digital devices for educational purpose can help a lot . Focus should also be given on General Lower Income class up to a certain level . Teachers should be trained on new methods of teaching and how they can make the subject interesting for students .

The Implementation process is a long one and its not going to be easy for the country . Although its quiet early to predict results , if this policy is implemented in an efficient way with certain changes , it can truly change the shape of educational system of the country and can make India an educational hub . These Pandemic times are challenging but should not be a hindrance in the effective Implementation of this policy because:-

"Life is about accepting the challenges along the way, choosing to keep moving forward, and savoring the journey."(3)

CHAPTER SIX

COMPARATIVE STUDY OF CONSUMER PROTECTION ACT (1986-2019)

Author: Ashutosh Verma, II year of B.A.,LL.B. from Faculty of Law, University of Lucknow

Introduction

The advanced age has guided and hugely filled in this new period of internet business and acquired its degree new assumptions and wants of the buyers. It has now gotten effectively open, with more extensive decisions to the purchasers and gives powerful strategies for business. Because of such an upset which is achieved by digitalization, the Consumer Protection Act, 1986 had a few difficulties and confronted numerous mishaps which required quick consideration. Yet, the public authority achieved an extraordinary change and presented the Consumer Protection Act, 2019 which came into power on 20 July 2020. This previous authorization had been overhauled from time to time to get it similar with changes achieved by globalization, financial progression, digitalization of items and administrations, and so forth, be that as it may, its execution was far to accomplish its ideal target of financial enactment which tried to give assurance of the interests of the buyers. While then again, the new Consumer Protection Act, 2019 will fortify and improve the extent of security given to the buyers by patching up the promoting claims, supports, disciplines, prison terms, organization of the questions, and different elements.

Consumer Protection Act, 1986

This act was passed by the Indian Parliament to secure consumer rights and to review consumer objections and resolve consumer debates. One might say that the act was based on the principle of caveat emptor i.e., let the buyer beware.This act provided consumers certain rights which were the right to be heard, the right to consumer education, the right to seek redressal against unfair trade practices, the right to be protected against hazardous products, and the right to be informed about the quality, price and etc of the products.

Furthermore, the Act also explained who consumer is and what right do they have. Aside from that is likewise states itemized arrangements identifying with the organization and settlement of the buyer questions through three-level quasi-judicial component at the District, State and National levels for redressal of customer complaints.

Consumer Protection Act, 2019

The amendment of 2019 to the Consumer Protection Act came following 33 years of the old act being passed. Innovation has advanced a ton in these years and keeping in mind that the more seasoned amendment attempted to keep refreshed with little alterations to a great extent.The Consumer Protection Act, 2019 brought significant changes to give more insurance to the purchasers and gave numerous new ideas like e commerce, product liability and etc. It can be said that the only purpose of this act is look after the interest after of the consumer and to give them speedy answers for their issues.

Comparative analysis of CPA 1986 and CPA 2019

Definition of Consumer

The Act of 1986 had the meaning of consumer restricted and did exclude the idea of ecommerce business, online transaction, etc. In contrast the Act of 2019 express that it incorporates all goods and services including housing development, telecom and all method of exchange, while barring free and individual assistance. In this way, the meaning of consumer from that point and presently got extended.

Pecuniary Jurisdiction

The Act of 1986 provided district form to take matter upto Rs. 20 lakhs, state commission could take matter concerning above Rs. 20 lakhs upto 1 crore and national commission would take above Rs. 1 crore.

However, with time the income of people and their shopping way of life has colossally developed throughout the timeframe. The sum which the people spend on their buy, projects, etc. was extremely insignificant when contrasted with 21st century. In the wake of new amendment, the Act of 2019 now enables district commission to take dispute worth doesn't surpass Rs. 1 crore. The state commission now can take dispute whose worth surpasses Rs. 1 crore yet doesn't surpass Rs. 10 crores and national commission can take dispute whose worth surpasses Rs. 10 crores.

Product Lability

The Act of 1986 didn't have any provision related to Product Lability. However, it is presented in the Act of 2019. This provision gives consumer the option to guarantee item responsibility for issues in goods and service against the product maker, service provider and product seller and if not met the same would have to be compensated. The fascinating part of the arrangements is that now the risk for the item is appended more towards the producers than the merchant and furthermore compensation can be acquired by demonstrating one of the few indicated conditions given in the 2019 Act.

Misleading Advertisement

Prior, if an individual docsn't follow requests of the Commissions, he might confront detainment between one month and three years or a fine between Rs 2,000 to Rs 10,000 or both. While presently in the new demonstration, 2019, he might confront detainment as long as three years, or a fine at the very least Rs 25,000 extendable to Rs one lakh, or both.

Independent Regulator

Prior, in 1986 there was no different power that could admire the complaints of consumers. Though, according to Section 10(1) of the Act 2019, the Central Consumer Protection Authority was set up. This authority was set up to manage matters identifying with encroachment of privileges of customers, and bogus or deluding of ads under the ambit of uncalled for exchange rehearses, likewise to advance and uphold the interest of consumers as a class. The Central Consumer Protection Authority likewise appreciates different forces to make managerial strides, for example, giving wellbeing sees, passing requests to review products, forestalling unreasonable exchange rehearses, re-remunerating price tag paid, forcing punishments for bogus or misdirecting notices, and capacities like, controlling, exploring, arbitrating at the same time.

Mediation

The act of 1986 had no such legitimate arrangement that could assist consumers with resolving down their disputes in time efficient way. Though, part V of the Act of 2019, acquainted an arrangement with guarantee quick resolution, where the court can allude for settlement through mediation.

Conclusion

The Consumer Protection Act is significant for the dealer just as for consumers. Due to deficient data present in the Act of 1986,it became fundamental for consumer protection to supplant and bring another Act of 2019.The new Act addresses numerous perspectives. Thus, it was critical to alter the act when digitalization has changed the manner in which a shopper goes through with online exchanges and the method of shopping has moved from offline to online.

Certainly 2019 Act is a positive advance towards reorganization, improvement, and upgrading buyer rights. However, the genuine execution of 2019 Act will be found in coming occasions by dissecting how much help it offers to the purchasers.

CHAPTER SEVEN

A DETAILED STUDY ON MALICIOUS PROSECUTION IN INDIA

Author: R.B.Sneha, II year of B.B.A.,LL.B. from Symbiosis Law School, Hyderabad

R.B.Sneha

Introduction

"Tort, in common law, civil law, and the vast majority of legal systems that derive from them, any instance of harmful behaviour, such as physical attack on one's person or interference with one's possessions or with the use and enjoyment of one's land, economic interests (under certain conditions), honour, reputation, and privacy"[1]. Tort is a latin word that is derived from the the word "tortum" it means to twist.

Malicious prosecution means mischievous prosecution against the another person for being prosecuted without any reasonable or probable cause that may cause the other defending party loss of their privilege, financial and reputation. There are many jurist who explained about malicious prosecution. "Malicious prosecution is the malicious institution of unsuccessful criminal or bankruptcy or liquidation proceedings against another without reasonable or probable cause. This tort balances competing principles, namely freedom that every person should have in bringing criminals to justice and the need for restraining false accusations against innocent persons."[2] In this offence the primary motive of the person committing the offence is for their selfishness they want to file a false suit on other without any reasonable cause.In Malicious Prosecution it is the duty of the plaintiff to prove that the reasonable cause was not present and the reasonable ground is not satisfied only then the damages can be recovered from the defendant.

Example:- When Hari tells Shyam (the police officer) to arrest Raju, but Shyam mistakes and arrest Ram instead of Raju. Hari tells Shyam to arrest even after knowing that Shyam is not arresting Raju. In this case Hari will be held liable for committing the offence of malicious prosecution.

What are the reasons that amounts to malicious Prosecution

- When a person is preparing an incorrect or a false documents and records and submitting it to the judicial proceedings.
- When bringing any instituted false criminal proceeding or any false charges against someone.
- Destroying all the important evidence in order not let the judicial know about the evidence and escape from the particular case.
- Making a person to commit trial acting or confinement to the contrary to law.

There will be compensation provided to the plaintiff when they go through Malicious prosecution but they need to prove on these following

- That the defendant had done malicious prosecution against the plaintiff
- That the present suit for the malicious prosecution is in the favour go the plaintiff
- That the malicious prosecution was instituted with any reasonable or probable cause
- The defendant had the malicious intention
- The damage that the plaintiff has suffered to his property or their reputation or safety of a person.
- The ingredients of Malicious Prosecution

- The plaintiff in the case should be prosecuted
- The defendant should be the prosecuted where the plaintiff has been prosecuted because of him

Related cases

"Ram v. Madan Gupta"[3] in this case the defendant falsely charged that plaintiff set fire in his house. Then they found that the plaintiff was innocent in this case and the defendant deliberately put the blame on the plaintiff. The plaintiff was awarded for his damages Rs:- 55,000 for loss of his privilege, financial loss and reputation.

"Vishweshwar Shankarrao Deshmukh and Anr v. Narayan VithobaPatil"[4], in this case the defendant filed a false complaint against the plaintiff that he was assaulting him when the defendant was performing his duty. The police then arrested the plaintiff and he was prosecuted for the charges of the false FIR. The court found that the plaintiff were innocent and they held the defendants liable for the malicious prosecution. The court made defendants compensate to plaintiff Rs.12500 for the loss of loss of his privilege, financial loss and reputation.

Research objective

- To understand the concept of malicious prosecution
- To know the elements of the malicious prosecution that is required by the plaintiff to prove for the damages of the suit.
- To analyse the Remedies and Defences that is available for Malicious Prosecution
- To examine malicious prosecution in India

Research Question

- What the the history of malicious Prosecution?
- What is the difference between Malice and Malicious Prosecution ?
- Who will be liable for the malicious prosecution
- What is the probable and reasonable cause involved in Malicious prosecution?

Literature Review

In the study while researcher doing her Preliminary study she has found that there isn't any article or researcher paper regarding the west Bengal case but they researcher has found various literature works about Malicious Prosecution.

"law of torts"[5]:- In this book the author has explained about malicious prosecution by referring to various Indian and English case laws. The author has also stated about what are the Intentions that is being Malicious prosecution and what are the damages because of it. This book is a very descriptive book where all the information has been displayed briefly. The author has explained detailed about the 5 essentials of the malicious prosecution. "Law of tort"[6] in this book the author has explained about malicious prosecution the malicious process that is involved with it by using various Indian and English case law. The author also mention five legal proceeding that will be used when there is malicious prosecution. Lastly the author also explained about malice that it means when there is a wrongful or improper motive to cause damage to the other.

"Malice as an Ingredient of tort liability"[7] this article is about malice and it stated the four torts that the malice is involved and the author draws conclusion between tort liabilities and malice.the author also stated that detailed explanation about Malice with the case.

"Law of Defamation and Malicious Prosecution"[8], this is an other book that explains about malicious prosecution and it is very descriptive and the also also stated c\various definition of malicious prosecution from various jurists. This really helped the researcher to analysis well on prosecution and the case.

<u>Malicious Prosecution and judicial interpretation with India and English Case laws</u>

The Evolution of Malicious Prosecution

The malicious prosecution has been evolved over ages ago and it was origin in English over the eighteenth and nineteenth century , this was an outcome of people missing the procedure of law in England . There were a lot of criminal proceeding where people were misusing the law for their own personal joy so because of this the malicious prosecution was evolved. Later it stated to spread to other countries around the world and this has become common wealth to the countries. "Malicious prosecution has also caught a very strong footing in the United States, probably because they hold the persons liberty and reputation in the highest regard. The American Courts have been liberal in interpreting the concept and it has thus established a strong existence in their legal eco system."[9]

Who will be liable for the malicious prosecution?

"The settled law in India is that the defendant is liable as prosecutor, if he filed a complaint himself or through his agent or advocate or, if the prosecution was by the police of the State, at his instance and on his information"[10]. The actual prosecutor will be not be liable for malicious prosecution because the police who is investigating the case will also be responsible equally has he will be knowing that he is constituting the case that is a malicious case. Also the witness will also be liable in the proceedings of the prosecution. The victim will be the person who will be getting claim for the damages that is caused by the defendant. If there is any statement that is made by the defendant in the investigation that suggests the witness names in the prosecution that has been examined, then it cannot be said that the defendant has influences the case against the witness.

Case laws

"A.Akkuliya v. Mattibu venataswami Naidu"[11], in this case the madras of High Court held that the proceeding are under Section 145 of the criminal Procedure code, when there is prosecution then the can be suit filed for damages and malicious prosecution would lie.

"Abarth vs north eastern railway"[12] in this case this was about a medical advisor who has recovered a huge amount of damages that is caused by the railways. After that the railways company ascertained certain facts before the council that Abarth and the other person have prosecuted a fraud to the company. The court held that Abarth was not prosecuted and he was acquitted. Abarth took an action against the company and filed for malicious Prosecution but the court held that the company is not liable has there was a probable and reasonable cause.

"S.T. Sahib v. Hasan Ghani"[13] in this case the court held that the malicious prosecution was a similar law in the England, on this subject the same is same as the USA and England.

"Madan Mohan Singh v. Bhrigunath Singh"[14] this case was about the person who got jail punishment for almost 40 days because he was charged for dacoity, but there was no congizance taken according to the offence so the judge stated that there was an prosecution act for the purpose of the action of malicious prosecution.

<u>Essential Elements of Malicious Prosecution</u>

1. The Malicious Prosecution is done by the Defendant:- this is a very essential element where the plaintiff should prove that the defendant has the malicious prosecution act in the suit for the damages. "Musa Yakum v.

Manilal"[15]in this case the court held that the defendant had no excuse that he has done the malicious prosecution act under the order of the court, if the defendant moved the court for his false evidence for an order.

2. When there is absence of the Probable and Reasonable cause:- when there is a need for a suit of damages by the plaintiff, the plaintiff should also prove that defendant has dome prosecution act without a probable and reasonable cause. A reasonable and probable cause will not be admissible once the prosecutor wishes to prosecute by ignoring that cause. If a prosecution is not carried out or if a prosecution acquits the accused of all charges, there can be no interpretation made on the existence or absence of reasonable and probable cause that resulted in such a decision.If an accused formally accepts several charges, allegations or accusations against him wherein some charges consist of a probable cause and some others don't, he will still be liable for malicious prosecution.

3. The act of the Defendant was maliciously:- when there is a need for a suit of damages by the plaintiff, the plaintiff is also required to prove that the defendant has acted maliciously while prosecuting him and he didn't have the intention to carry the law into effect. Malice is not done with the feeling of vengeance or enmity but the purpose of malicious can be improper for the prosecutor to gain a beneficial advantage. "Bank of India v. Lekshmi Das"[16] in this case the court held that in the Malice act should be proved that there is absence of the Probable and Reasonable cause. In certain cases it is not necessary that from the start of the prosecution the defendant should have acted malicious prosecution. When the prosecutor is innocent in the starting and then when he becomes malicious then the action of the malicious prosecution becomes a lie.

4. The Termination of the proceeding are in the favour of the plaintiff:- when there is a need for a suit of damages by the plaintiff for malicious prosecution, it is mandatory that termination of proceeding are in the favour of the plaintiff. In the termination of proceeding in the favour of the plaintiff this does not mean there is absence of judicial determination because of his innocence. There can be no actions that can be brought when the proceeding or the prosecution is still pending because according to the rule of law that any allege should not be allowed in any pending suits and that is unjust. "It is essential to show that the proceeding alleged to be instituted has terminated in favour of the plaintiff, if, from its nature, it be capable of such a termination.The reason seems to be that, if in the proceeding complained of the decision was against the plaintiff and was

unreversed; it would not be consistent with the principles on which law is administered, for another court, not being a court of Appeal, to hold that the decision had come to without reasonable and probable cause.The plaintiff need not prove an acquittal, for a prosecution may be determined in various ways, or his innocence"[17].

5. The Plaintiff should have suffered damaged because of the malicious act which is done by the Defendant:- while the plaintiff filing a suit for the damages there should prosecution that the plaintiff had suffered. If the plaintiff wants to claim for damages then the damages should be:

- There should be damages to the reputation of the plaintiff
- There should be a damage to plaintiff's person
- There should be a damage to the property of the plaintiff

Detailed Analysis on the case " West Bengal State of Electricity Board v. Dilip Kumar Ray"[18]

Detailed facts of the case

This case was about Dilip Kumar who was the respondent who worked in the West Bengal elecrticity board has the superintending Engineer. He was suspended from his work without any reason. So Dilip filed a writ petition against them in the Calcutta Hight Court tasing for a preceding of what is the reason for his suspension. The court asked the electricity board to produce the charge sheet and they produced the charge sheet with 10 allegations against him. The resonant filed another writ petition stated that the allegation were false, then the court appointed an officer to investigate the matter.

The investigation officer couldn't establish all the allegation made against the respondent but there are certain allegation that was true with proof. The respondent stated in the court that he was not given an opportunity to be heard in the investigation and he was not allowed to access or check the document which was pre adjudicating his defence. The court held in the favour of the respondent and order the appellant to pay salary in arrears.

The respondent filed a new civil suit before the District Judge because the proceeding of the writ petition was dismissed in Hight court and claimed for damages because of the false allegations made. The trial held that the respondent should receive Rs.50,000 for the for losing his reputation and another Rs.50,000 for the mental harassment made against him. However the court did not mention anything about Malicious Prosecution.

However the appellants appealed to the high court and the high court interpreted the decision of the lower court in a different way. High court heck that there was malicious prosecution and that was the reason of mental harassment to the respondent and for the damages the appellant should give Rs.50,000. The appellants appealed to the supreme court because the high court was contradicting the lower court about the an evidence to prove malicious prosecution was present. The supreme court gave a detailed definition of malicious prosecution that "Malicious Prosecution – Malice. If the defendant had reasonable or probable cause of launching the criminal prosecution no amount of malice will make him liable for damages. Reasonable and probable cause must be such, as would operate on the mind of a discreet and reasonable man; malice and want of reasonable and probable cause have reference to the state of the defendant's mind at the date of the initiation of criminal proceedings and the onus rests on the plaintiff to prove them."[19]

Case Analysis and Case comment

The supreme court of India have very well explained about malicious prosecution in the case West Bengal State of Electricity Board(appellant) against Dilip Kumar Ray(respondant)

Firstly there was a writ petition that was filed by the respondent in the high court of Calcutta because of his suspension of his work in West Bengal State of Electricity Board without issuing a charge sheet within 4 months. According to law a public servant should receive a charge sheet for his suspension within the reasonable time.Referring to this case "Firestone Tyre & Rubber Co. Ltd. v. Their worknen 1967 LLJ - 11 717 that Non-issuance of charge sheet in disciplinary proceedings would amount to prejudice against the delinquent and considered unfair" the high court told the board to issue the charge sheet. There was various allegations that was made by the electricity board to the respondent and respondent said that its also allegation and then the court appointed a investigation officer. The investigation officer had stated that the charges 1, 4, 6, 7, 8 and 9 are false has there is no proof and Charges 2, 5, and 10 are true and Charge 3 is might be true, the court held that the respondent should be given salary arrears and the respondent should his work . Since the respondent was not satisfied has he lost his reputation with the investigation he filed a new suit to the district judge. Similarly in the case "Addis v. Gramophone Company

Ltd"[20] the company suspending Addis the employee which was very 'harsh and humiliating', so court held in the favour of respondent because loss of reputation and can claim for his damages. So the court held the same decision in current case.

The appellants were not sataified so they made an appeal to the high court of Calcutta, but the high court up held the decision of the lower court in a different interpretation that they while they were converging the harassment there was malicious prosecution emerging, hence the respondent is entitled to receive Rs.50,000 for his damages.

The appellants weren't again satisfied with the decision so they filed an appeal to seek a remedy in the Supreme Court. The appellants contented their reasons for the damages to the supreme and the supreme court held the definition of 'malice' and 'malicious prosecution'.

Conclusion and Suggestion

Conclusion

Malicious act is not with a intention to The main 5 elements of malicious procession is Malicious Prosecution is done by the Defendant, absence of the Probable and Reasonable cause, act of the Defendant was maliciously, Termination of the proceeding are in the favour of the plaintiff and The Plaintiff suffered damaged because of malicious act by the Defendant . The supreme court has briefly explained about 'malicious prosecution' and 'malice' in Dilip Kumar case If the plaintiff wants to claim compensation for the damages then he need to prove the essential of malicious prosecution.Only the court has the decision to say that if the suit filed by the plaintiff for damages is because malicious Prosecution or not.

Suggestions

The government should bring strict laws to prevent from malicious prosecution because no one can misuse the procedures of the law and they should be punished.

CHAPTER EIGHT

PROBATION UNDER SERVICE LAWS

<u>Author</u>: Varnit Vashistha, IV year of B.A.,LL.B. from Maharaja Aggrasen Institute of Management Studies, GGSIPU

Varnit Vashistha

Abstract

In Indian Labour Law there are no provisions that define the term "PROBATION". Probation as the term suggests is a period in which an employer can check whether the newly appointed person is suitable for the post or not and whether he or she is fulfilling the required expectations/ standard for the said post and check whether if he or she should be permanently appointed or not. The basic idea behind keeping an employee on probation by the employer is to evaluate the employee for the post on which he or she is to appointed. Some employers are under the incorrect assumption that, by appointing a new employee under probation, it entitles them to use probation as an excuse to fire the employee if he/she does not fit in (as example only), without having to meet formal legal obligations.Consequently, it is clear that so long as an employee is on probation, continuation of his or her employment is not certain, and is subject to the employer being satisfied that the employee is suitable for the job. Thus, all the terms and conditions should be carefully kept in mind by both the employer and the employee.

KEYWORDS: EMPLOYER, EMPLOYEE, PROBATION, OBLIGATIONS

INTRODUCTION

1. A person is appointed on probation in order to evaluate his or her eligibility for absorption in the service on which he or she has been appointed. Probation should not, therefore, be treated as a mere formality. No formal declaration is required for in respect of appointment on probation. The employer can declare on successful completion or extend the period of probation or terminate the services on the basis of his or her evaluation of performance.

2. Probation is mainly put in practice when there is direct recruitment, promotion from one group to another or for officers re-employed before the age of superannuation. The probation shall stand successfully completed upon issue of orders in writing.

3. Instead of treating probation as a formality, the existing powers to discharge probationers should be systematically and vigorously used to the necessity of dispensing with the services of employees at later stages may arise only rarely.

4. Concentration of attention should be there on the probationer's ability to pass the probationary or departmental examinations, and if applicable then it should play an important role in confirmation of the candidate. Also, a very careful assessment of the outlook, aptitude and character for the kind of work that he or she has done before the probationer is confirmed.

5. A probationer should be given an opportunity to work under different officers and his performance report should be accumulated from each of those officers. These probation reports which are for the whole period will be taken into consideration when confirming the position of probationer. For this purpose separate forms of reports are to be used which are distinct

from the Annual Performance Appraisal Report (APAR) forms. The probation period reports, unlike APAR, are written to help the supervising officer to concentrate on the special needs of probation and to decide whether the work and conduct of the officer during the period of probation or the extended period of probation are satisfactory enough to warrant his further retention in service or post. The probation period reports thus do not serve the purpose for which the APARs are written and vice versa. Therefore, in the case of all probationers or officers on probation, separate probation period reports should be written in addition to the usual APARs for the period of probation.

6. A probation should not extended for more than one year and in no case an employee should be kept in probation for more than double the normal period.

7. If a probationer is not making progress in his work then he or she should be informed of the shortcomings in his work so that he or she can make additional efforts well before the expiry of probationary period. This can be done by giving him or her a written warning with reference to the fact that his or her performance have not been up to the expectations and if they don't show substantial improvement within a specific period of time then the employer may consider discharging them of their duties.

8. During the period of probation, the candidates may be required to do specific training and instructions and pass examinations as the Employee may deem fit as a condition for the satisfactory completion of probation.

RULES AND REGULATIONS RELATING TO PROBATION PERIOD

Period of probation prescribed for different posts/services in Central Government:

S.NO.	METHOD OF APPOINTMENT	PERIOD OF PROBATION
	PROMOTION	
1.	PROMOTION FROM ONE GRADE TO ANOTHER BUT WITHIN IN THE SAME GROUPS OF POSTS e.g. from group "c" to group "c"	NO PROBATION
2.	PROMOTING FROM ONE GROUP TO ANOTHER e.g. "group c" to "group d"	The probation should be prescribed by the senior officials and if not so then the period should be of 2 years.
	DIRECT RECRUITMENT	
3.	i. For direct recruitments except clause (ii) below ii. For direct recruitment to posts carrying a Grade Pay of ₹7600 or above or to the post where maximum age is 35 years and where no training is involved	2 YEARS 1 YEAR
4.	Officers re-employed before the age of superannuation	2 YEARS
5.	Appointment on contract basis, tenure basis, re-employment after superannuation and absorption	NO PROBATION

RIGHTS OF A PROBATIONER

1. A probationer shall be entitled to leave under the provisions of the Rule 33 of the CCS (Leave) Rules, 1972. If, for any reason, it is proposed to terminate the services of a probationer, any leave which may be granted to him shall not extend; I. beyond the date on which the probationary period

as already sanctioned or extended, expires, or II. beyond any earlier date on which his services are terminated by the orders of an authority competent to appoint him.

2. Employees on probationary period enjoy same rights as the other staff. They are as follows:

i. Receive at least the National Minimum Wage or National Living Wage (depending on their age)

ii. Itemized payslips

iii. Paid holiday entitlement which will begin to accumulate from the first day of employment

iv. Maximum working hours and minimum breaks

v. Maternity leave

3. As far as the matter of maternity leave is concerned, it should not be granted ordinarily during the probation period until or unless some extreme situation arises and the leave sanctioning authority is fully satisfied regarding the need for maternity leave to the probationer.

4. Joining Time is granted to the Government servants on transfer in public interest. The period of joining time availed by a probationer on return from leave should be counted towards the prescribed period of probation if but for leave, he or she would have continued to officiate in the post to which he or she was appointed.

<u>EXTENSION OF PROBATION PERIOD</u>

1. The probation period is extended only when a probationer has not undergone any requisite training course or passed the departmental examination (proficiency in Hindi etc.), if there is an extension in probation period then it should be kept in mind that the period of probation should not exceed double the prescribed period of probation.

2. If the appointing authority deems fit then they can extend the probation period by a specific period and it should not exceed double the normal period. In the extended probation period, periodic reviews are to be done and the extension should not be for a long time.

3. hen a probationer has completed the term of his probation up to the satisfactions of the employer then he should confirmed for the post at the end of probation period.

4. If an employee has not completed his or her probation due to taking leave for long duration and if he has not completed his 75% of his probation period then the extension should be given only of the period which he has missed. And it should be kept in mind that it should not exceed double the

original period.

TERMINATION OF PROBATION

1. When the employer is not satisfied with the performance of the employee on probation then the employer is free to terminate the probationer by giving him a notice. The decision regarding confirmation of the employee should be taken within six to eight weeks of after the expiry of initial probationary period.

2. After the expiry of probationary period efforts should be made to obtain the assessment report of the probationer so as to:

Confirm his or her position or issue orders regarding the satisfactory termination of the probationer

Extend the period of probation or discharge the probationer or terminate him or her in accordance with the relevant rules and regulations given by the competent authority, if the probationer has not completed his or her term satisfactorily

3. Timely action is required as to avoid the delay in confirmation.

4. If it ever comes to notice of appointing authority during the period of probation that the probationer is not making substantive efforts then he or she can be reverted back to the post preceding their appointment.

5. A probationer reverted or discharged does not have any right to be entitled to any compensation.

LEGAL ISSUES REGARDING TERMINATION

CASE: Chaitanya Prakash and Anr. Vs. H. Omkarappa [(2010)2SCC623] Facts of this case are

In this case the respondent was offered an appointment to post of Executive Director [Marketing] by the Appellant no. 2 which goes by the name of, M/s. Hindustan Photo Films Manufacturing Company Ltd. by issuing an offer of appointment dated 03.06.1998. The appointment was made with the condition that respondent will be on probation for a period of one year which can be extended too.

During the period of your employment in the Company, you will be governed by the Service Rules of Hindustan Photo Films Service Rules for Officers, which would be applicable to the officers of the company as may be in force from time to time.

Clause-3 of the Hindustan Photo Films Service Rules for Officers which came into effect on 1st March, 1974 deals with matter of probation. The relevant sub- clauses within clause-3, read as follows:

"3.1 An Officer appointed by direct recruitment or promotion shall be on probation for a period of one year from the date of joining the post. 3.2 The performance during the period of probation shall be reviewed by the Company and the Company may extend the period of probation or terminate the services of the probationer recruited from outside at any time during or at the time of the probation period."

After this the performance of the respondent was came under scrutiny and the appointing authority was not satisfied with his work and his probation was by another three months.

ISSUE

The issue that falls for consideration in this appeal is whether the impugned order passed by the appellants against the respondent terminating his service during the period of probation was an order of termination simpliciter due to unsatisfactory service or "stigmatic" due to misconduct.

HELD

In this case the Hon'ble Court held that the termination order referring to the unsatisfactory services of the probationer cannot be said to be stigmatic and there is no need to follow the principles of natural justice while terminating the services of a probationer.

CASE: Shri Syed Mohiuddin Ashraf &Anr. Vs. M/s. Central Electronics Limited (2013)

In this case too a similar issue has been contended by the petitioners that their orders of termination were void as they are violative of principles of natural justice, arbitrary, stigmatic and punitive in nature and without any reason as the petitioners had rendered satisfactory services. In the present case, the Hon'ble Court brushed aside the contentions taken by the petitioners and it was held that the principles of natural justice need not be followed while terminating the services of a probationary officer. In so far as the plea of stigmatic order is concerned, the Hon'ble court observed that since the orders of termination only states that petitioners are unfit for continuing their work thus, the expression used in the order cannot be said as stigmatic in nature.

CONCLUSION

The Probationer remains a Probationer until the company decides and communicate the decision to the employee within the reasonable time period regarding the extension of the probation period. If the work is not satisfactory then the Probation is extended or else he or she is terminated by the employee.

However, to avoid disputes, one must provide for a specific action without which the employee shall not be deemed to be confirmed. Care needs to be taken while drafting employment letters and company policies. Also if an employer discharges an employee on the basis of misconduct then there is a nexus between misconduct and discharge and the order of termination is not stigmatic and a departmental enquiry may be imperative.

CHAPTER NINE

ANALYSING THE OUTER SPACE TREATY IN THE LIGHT OF RISING SPACE TOURISM

Author: Shubhi Pandey, IV year of B.B.A.,LL.B. from Symbiosis Law School, Noida

The Outer Space Treaty marked its 54th anniversary on 10th October 2021 and during all these years, the field of space and technology has witnessed development at an exponential rate. The last decade has decade has opened a new arena of space tourism. In 1967, when the Outer Space Treaty was signed, the space arena was dominated by a very few countries (such as Russia and The US). But in past 54 years, almost every country has registered its presence in this arena. Recently, business tycoons like Elon Musk and Jeff Bezos have provided a commercial angle to this field by launching rockets and satellite for the purpose of private space tourism. With such advancements in the field, the major issue that comes to one's mind is whether the Outer Space Treaty has the capacity to govern such advancements or does it need a reformation or replacement.

Now, if one dives into the analysis of the current situation of space tourism, one could easily point out how the numbers of commercial rockets (i.e. the rockets made and launched by private companies) are increasing in the outer space. SpaceX alone has sent more than 800 satellites last year. Many private space companies have started monetizing the space tourism by making it accessible to the general public. But, while getting familiar with the idea of space tourism, one needs to understand whether the grundnorm of the same has the ability to cope up with this tangent of the field. The Outer Space Treaty has already declared the space as a "demilitarized zone" and has also declared the moon and other celestial bodies as "province of all mankind". But, does this include private entities and imposes a liability on those? In order to find an answer to that question, one needs to refer to Article VI and VII of the treaty.

Article VI of the treaty has clearly put an international liability on the party states for every national activity that is being carried out by them. In order to understand this better, one could take the example of a space entity that is owned by the government of a party state, such as NASA. Now, USA as a party state would be held internationally liable for any space activity conducted by NASA. Article VI further adds that this liability has to be borne by the party state in case of "both governmental and non-governmental organisations". Now, the term "non-governmental organisations" would automatically include the private space companies. For instance, the government of United States would also be internationally liable for the activities conducted by SpaceX, Blue Origin etc. Article VI further adds that such activities being conducted by the private entities have to be carried out under "authorization and continuing supervision" of the concerned part state. This means that companies like SpaceX and Blue Origin will have to seek authorization of the US government in order to carry out their space operations. This approach of Article VI could be interpreted in two ways. The first way involves critical analyses of the treaty because it puts the entire liability on the states and no liability on the private companies. It simply refers to "non-governmental entities" which is a very broad term and it does not put a cap on the activities of such companies. This could also be due to the uncertainty in the field of scientific developments in 1967. The treaty is also silent upon the space traffic and rising space debris which could cause a lot of problems as both governmental and private entities continue to send their rockets/satellites in the space without a limit. This may result into jamming, spoofing etc.

The other way of interpreting this clause could be by looking into its jurisprudence. It might be considered that the framers of this treaty wanted the party states to act like a parent (doctrine of parens patriae) so that they could form their own laws with respect to private entities as well and could set up a limit by themselves. Ever since the idea of commercialisation of space has come up, countries like the US have been framing laws in the same direction (The US Government passed a law titled "Commercial Space

Launch Competitiveness Act, 2015" which allowed commercialisation of space and also allowed activities like mining on the moon and mars).Article VII of the treaty compliments Article VI as it imposes an international liability on the party states in case of any damaged caused. It could be assumed from this article that such a liability would be borne by the party state for the damage caused by both government and private entities. Therefore, it could be said that the citizens of any party state would be acting on the behalf of their country.

After connecting the provisions laid down under the Outer Space Treaty with rising space tourism and commercialisation of space, it could be assumed that the makers of the treaty left it in an ambiguous state intentionally so that the same might cover the unforeseen technological advancements. Though, many countries have started passing regulations related to rising space tourism for both research and commercial purposes. But, with such advancement, there is a need for a new international regulation that also addresses the issueof commercialisation of space so as to prevent harsh consequences (both foreseeable and unforeseen) of the same.

Author's Biography

Ms.Shubhi Pandey is currently pursuing B.B.A. LL.B. from Symbiosis Law School, NOIDA. She has a keen interest in Public International Law, Environmental Law and Energy Law and has volunteered with organizations such as Wildlife S.O.S. India, Balrampur Chini Mills Ltd. etc in the domain of environmental and energy law compliance and aims to continue her practice in the aforementioned fields after her graduation.

CHAPTER TEN

CITIZENSHIP AMENDMENT ACT, 2019

Author: Vipul Solanki, II year of B.B.A.,LL.B. from BM Law College, Jodhpur
Co-author: Aditi Vyas, II year of B.B.A.,LL.B. from BM Law College, Jodhpur

A citizen of a state is person who enjoys full civil and political rights. Citizenship carries with it certain advantages given by the constitution. There are two types of people in country, one is a citizen and another is an alien. Aliens do not enjoy the rights given by the constitution. There are certain fundamental rights available to the citizens given by the constitution.

The constitution in its Part II covers the definition of citizenship. Article 5 to article 11 covers the citizenship. Citizenship on the commencement of the Constitution i.e., January 26, 1950. People falling under the article 5 to 8 of the Indian constitution shall be citizen of India at commencement of constitution

1. Citizenship by domicile (Article 5): Article 5 entitles to citizenship by domicile if the person at commencement of the constitution has his domicile in India and secondly, either he was born in India or one of his parents was born in India or he must have been a resident in India for not less than five years before the commencement of the constitution

2. Citizenship of emigrants from Pakistan (article 6): People who have migrated from Pakistan have been divided into two categories for purpose of citizenship, (i) those who came to India before July 19, 1948; (ii) those who came to India after July 19, 1948. This article provides that a migrant from Pakistan is deemed to be a citizen of India at the commencement of the constitution if he or either of his grandparents or parents were born in India and also must fulfil the conditions which apply in the following two

cases:

- If he migrated to India before July 19, 1948, he has been residing in India since the date of his migration
- If he migrated to India after July 19, 1948, and has been registered as Indian Citizen by an officer appointed by the government of India.

3. Citizenship of migrants to Pakistan (Article 7): Under article 7a,a citizen by domicile or by migration,gets his citizenship terminated if he has migrated to Pakistan after March 1, 1947, though there are exceptions in favor of a person who has returned to India on the basis of permit for resettlement in India.

4. Citizenship of Indians Aroid (Article 8): Article 8 provides that any person or either of whose parents or any of those grand-parents was born in India as defined in the Government of India Act,1935, and who is ordinarily residing in any country outside India, shall be deemed to be a citizen of India as if he has been registered as a citizen of India by the Diplomatic or Consular representative of India in the country where he is for the time being residing, on an application made by him to such representative before or after 26 Jan 1950 in the manner prescribed by the Government of Dominion of India.

Citizenship Amendment Acts

In the Citizenship act of 1995, the act provided rules for determination and acquisition of the Indian citizenship. It also allows the people who were once a citizen of India and are now residing in another country to provide and Overseas citizens of India Card. This act of Indian citizenship has till date been amended for 6 times, in 1986, 1992, 2003, 2015, and the latest in 2019 which created a very bad scenario in the countries with protests carrying out nation-wide.

In the 1986 amendments of the amendment was made that to acquire the citizenship either of the parents must be a citizen of India during the time of birth

The 1992 amendment stated that person born outside India shall be a citizen of India by descent, on or after January 26, 1950, but before December 10, 1992, if his father is a citizen of India at the time of his birth.

The 2003 amendments introduced to us a new term "illegal immigrants" and also Made the government to conduct a National Registrant of Citizens. This amendment inserted the Section 14A for the headcount of Indian

Citizens and Conduction of NRC in the country.

IN the 2005 amendment the government made provisions for the people residing of the country of Indian origin by introducing the concept of Person of Indian Origin (PIO) and overseas citizens of India (OCI) which granted them certain limited rights of a citizen.

The 2015 amendment introduced the concept of an 'Overseas Citizen of India Cardholder' (an "OCC") that essentially replaced and merged OCIs and PIOs. The merging of the two schemes provided PIO cardholders the benefits extended to OCIs, such as visa-free travel to India, rights of residency and participation in business and educational activities in the country.

The new citizenship act, 2019 made provisions for the illegal immigrants of six communities from Pakistan, Afghanistan, and Bangladesh to apply for citizenship and certain other provisions discussed further in the article.

Citizenship Amendment Act, 2019

According to this act Hindus, Christians, Sikhs, Jains, Parsi and Buddhists who have entered India Illegally or without a valid visa on or before December 31, 2014 from the Muslim majority countries Pakistan, Afghanistan, Bangladesh and have stayed in the country for 5 years or more are eligible to apply for citizenship.

The refugees from the six religions (Sikhs, Buddhists, Jain, Parsi, Christian, Hindus) will be given citizenship after residence of 5 years now instead of 11 years, stated by the act. This act made provisions for these six religions that they be granted Indian citizenship from the date they entered India after 31st December 2014 and all the legal proceedings against them for being an illegal immigrant be closed. The bills also provide that these provisions will not be applicable for the tribes of Meghalaya, Assam,Mizoram, or Tripura, as included in the Sixth Schedule to the Constitution. Also, it will not be applicable on the areas under the Inner Line[i]. Immigrants from other countries such as Hindu from Sri Lanka and Muslims (Rohingya) from Myanmar are not included in this act.

This act is one of the most controversial and one of the most disliked acts by the Indian citizens. There are nationwide protests going against the passing of this act.

Changes Made for the OCI card

In the act passed in 1955 it was provided that the registration of the OCI card holder may get cancelled by the government on certain grounds., now in the new amendment the registrations can be called off on the grounds of violation of any laws provided by the government. Also, the order for the cancellation cannot be passed until the violator is being heard. This change can prove to excessive delegation of power by the legislation to the government to decide the laws on whose basis the registration of OCI card holder may get cancelled.

The bill has also not provided any limits or guidance on the government passing out the rules to be followed, which is violative of The Supreme court's order that while delegating powers to theexecutive authority, the legislature must prescribe a rule, standard, or policy for their guidance, that will set limits on the authority's powers and not give them arbitrary discretion to decide how to frame the rules.[ii]

Why these new provisions?

In India we do have other good provisions for providing citizenships to people, but the provisions are for providing citizenship to people who migrated legally, i.e., using a valid visa[iii]. Migrants which cross the border without any proper paperwork are not given citizenship and are even prosecuted for the same. According to the government, the need for this provision was to provide citizenship to the illegal non-Muslim immigrants who were not treated properly in the neighboring countries. The Muslims had other Islamic countries for their support but there was no country providing support to the non-Muslim communities.

Government says that these minority groups have come escaping oppression in Muslim-majority countries. However, the logic is not consistent – the bill does not protect all religious minorities, nor does it apply to all neighbors. The Ahmadi Muslim sect and even Shia's face discrimination in Pakistan. Rohingya Muslims and Hindus face persecution in neighboring Burma, and Hindu and Christian Tamils in neighboring Sri Lanka

Nation-wide protests

The nationwide protest is being carried out by two different types of groups one is by the north east states like Assam and Arunachal Pradesh, etc. as they fear that he there will be a rush of Bengali Hindu migrants from Bangladeshwhich will disturb their geographic, cultural and linguistic uniqueness, they don't care about the other reasons. And the other protests are being carried out in the other states of India, due to exclusion of the Muslim community as it being against the constitution.

CAA 2019: "Unconstitutional and anti-muslim"?

This is a very controversial topic, as everyone stands a different take on the constitutionality of the act. After analyzing in detail one can say that this act is violation of the Section 14[iv] of the Indian Constitution as it excludes the Muslim immigrants residing in the country. The basis of providing citizenship is by proper documentation such as property papers, birth certificates. In a country like India, whose more than half of the population is still below the poverty line, it would be difficult for the poor Muslims to have a proper documentation in their hands, the other poor communities won't be affected by it as they would be granted citizenship under this act. This act is clearlyviolating the provisions of Section 14 the Constitution of India which guarantees equality to each individual regardless of their religion, caste, creed, etc. but this act excludes the Muslim community on the basis of religion.

Governments take on the protests and the act being called unconstitutional

The government states that these six religions are being persecuted in the Muslim-majority nation and that they need to be protected from the persecution. On the other hand, there are Islamic nations for the Muslim communities to go. The governments states that there are no other countries for these religions that would provide shelters and refuge to them.

However, the government has still not answered the questions on including the Hindus and Christians minorities in Sri Lanka, Rohingya Muslims and Hindus which face persecution in Burma.

Conclusion

Citizenship amendment act, 2019, in my opinion is unconstitutional as it clearly violates article 14 of the Indian Constitution which guarantees equality to every person regardless of their race, caste, creed. There are some Muslims communities which face persecution even in the Islamic countries like the Ahmadis Muslim in Pakistan. There is an ordinance made in constitution of Pakistan which restrict the freedom of religion for the Ahmadis, they cannot call themselves Muslims or pose as Muslims which is punishable under three years of imprisonment. Another example is of the Rohingyas in Myanmar, the security forces in Myanmar have driven the Rohingyas off their land, burned down their mosques and committed rape of Rohingya Muslims. This proves that this act is biased against the Muslims, which the government defends by stating that for the Muslim minorities they have an option to move to the Islamic countries and that the other religious communities need to be protected from the persecution they face in the Islamic neighboring countries. Here in this act only the communities from Pakistan, Afghanistan and Bangladesh are taken into consideration stating that those communities face discrimination but, in Sri Lanka, the Tamilians and even the Hindus are not being treated well, then why those people are not being safeguarded, is still a big question-mark. Many PIL's are pending in the Supreme Court of India, the results of which will prove as it being unconstitutional or not.

CHAPTER ELEVEN

TRAIL SMELTER ARBITRATION (UNITED STATES v. CANADA) 1941, U.N. REP. INT'L ARB. AWARDS 1905 (1949)

Author: Saumya Sakshi, V year of B.A.,LL.B. from Amity Law School, Noida, UP

PARTIES: United States of America, Canada.

SPECIAL AGREEMENT: Convention of Ottawa, April 15, 1935.

ARBITRATORS: Charles Warren (U.S.A.), Robert A. E. Greenshields (Canada), Jan Frans Hostie (Belgium).

AWARD: April 16, 1938, and March 11, 1941.

INTRODUCTION

The Trail Smelter arbitration of 1938 and 1941 is considered as one of the historical decisions dealing with a dispute over environmental degradation between the United States and Canada. This Case deals with the issue of International Environmental Law. The crux of this case, there was damage was caused by one country to the environment of the other country that resulted in the legal suit. Legally, this issue was not taken as different from loss caused to the public or private property, for instance by the inadvertent penetration of a foreign State's territory by armed forces.

In this case for the very first time an international tribunal set out the principle that one country must not by itself, or by its national, let its territory used in such a manner that it causes trouble or harm to neighbouring countries. The tribunal announced a landmark decision where, it was propounded that damage would be provided in case there is an injury caused by one state to another state, even when there is no such existing treaty between the nations that provide an obligation to prevent such damage.

FACTS OF THE CASE

The Trail smelter is located at Trail, in British Colombia (Canada), this area is also known as a mineral-rich area. It was operated by the Consolidated Mining and Smelting Company COMINCO, in 2001 it merged with Teck. The smoke from these smelters was alleged to cause damage to trees, crops and land in the surrounding area and also border shared between Canada-US in Washington. The company without any interruption was operating the smelter and made it one of the largest and biggest smelting plant in the whole American continent.

Everything was going smooth, but in the year 1925 and 1927, the company raises its output increasing more sulphur dioxide fumes which distressed residents of nearby areas, resulting in complaints to COMINCO and demands for compensation.

The dispute resulted in a legal suit between the USA and Canada which was being sent to an arbitration tribunal. The USA was provided compensation of $350,000 in respect of damage caused till 1 January 1932 as recommended by the International Joint Commission. But the USA was unsatisfied with this and informed Canada about the same, thus an arbitral tribunal was set up to decide the issue finally. The Negotiation and resulting litigation and arbitration were finally settled in the year 1941.

ISSUE

The issue before the tribunal was that-

1. Is the state responsible for the damages caused to another country, due to harmful acts by its citizens from the jurisdiction of the country itself at all times?

2. Whether the smelter should be required to cease operation.

JUDGEMENT

Yes. The state is made responsible to protect other nations from damage caused due to harmful acts of individuals from the jurisdiction of the country at all times. In this case, Canada was held responsible and ordered to pay compensation to the USA for causing damage and was made obliged to reduce the pollution. While delivering the decision the tribunal made a landmark declaration which is often cited as precedent in any case that

"Under the principles of international law, as well as of the law of the United States, no State has the right to use or permit the use of its territory in such a manner as to cause injury by fumes in or to the territory of another or the properties or persons therein, when the case is of serious consequence and the injury is established by clear and convincing evidence." [i]

The tribunal also directed the trial smelter company to abate producing pollution as long as the pollution level is high in Washington, USA. The amount of damage paid is to be determined by the government of both countries according to article 3 of the convention that exists between these two countries.

At last, the tribunal provides a list of measures to control the pollution emission from the operation of a smelter, as in the opinion of the tribunal it may be possible in future that again damage may be caused due to operation of smelter unless they are controlled and curtailed.

RATIONAL

The rationale behind the judgement is that no nation is allowed to use or permit to use its territory in such a way that it causes damage to another nation. This is against the rule of international law, every state shall have to respect and take care of neighbouring states. And in this case, injury caused due to activity caused at the jurisdiction of a state, which causes loss to the person and properties of another state it is not allowed both in international law and the laws of the united stated.

The decision of trial smelter has founded the important principle underlying international environmental law. This principle provided that, A country will be held liable, if it creates transboundary pollution or any environmental hazardous effect which cause damage to another country, either directly or indirectly.

CHAPTER TWELVE

SITUATION IN NAGALAND

Author: Tejesh Bissa, I year of B.A.,LL.B. from BM law college, Jodhpur, Rajasthan

Tensions have increased in the Moan district of Nagaland since 4th December 2021 after a clash broke out between para commandoes and citizens of Nagaland because of which Section 144 CrPC that is; prohibiting the gathering of four or more people in a specified area, has been imposed. Leading to which the famous Hornbill Festival of Nagaland has also been called off.

On the evening of 5th December 2021, the army had set up an ambush based on credible intelligence of likely movements of insurgents of the Konyak terror group. A specific operation was planned to be conducted in the area of Tiru village of Moan district. But according to the complaint filed by villagers in the police station, they alleged that the "intention" of the security forces was to 'murder and injure civilians.' It is to be noted that there was no police guide nor did the army personnel make any requisition to the police station. Hence it was obvious according to the villagers that security forces intend to murder and injure civilians. But we need to keep in mind that during these operations of ambushes related to central government the security forces try not to involve regional police forces as it has been seen in many cases of terrorists like in, the Chota Rajan case in Maharashtra, where the officers under Ajit Doval had strategically tried to start a gang war between goons of Chota Rajan and some other gangsters but were stopped by regional police of Maharashtra, as a sense of community lies among the people of the same region.

The army personnel add to the situation when the vehicle carrying coal miners who were thought to be insurgents were asked to stop the vehicle. They denied doing so and the personnel in a sudden reaction attacked them. By the time the personnel reached the headquarters the news of killing was spread like fire and the office of Assam Riffles was surrounded by angry villagers protesting about the situation during which a soldier was also killed. The army to protect themselves again fired and killed more people.

Thus, killing 13 civilians and 1 soldier. While discussing the situation in Nagaland again the question arises in minds of many people why is this a topic of concern, aren't these types of killings common in these places?

Well, if anybody is having these types of thoughts in their minds then it is high time to know and understand about the unity of India and what bounds it. Can you think of a situation where these soldiers would have killed 13 civilians in Delhi what kind of reaction would you express and expect from the community would it be similar to the situation in Nagaland?

But still, why is this a topic of so much importance that the union home minister had to address the situation to the Prime Minister in the ongoing session. For this, we need to learn and understand the history of Nagaland and why the people within feel separated from India. In 1826, the British occupied the Assam region and started to use the land and labourers for their benefit. In the 1880s some protesting Naga labourers who were against the policies of the British started to work for the upliftment of their communities and formed Naga Labour Corporation and things were going smoothly. Later, during the 2nd World War, the Labour Corporation felt exploited by the British so they developed and formed Naga Club which after independence was declared as Naga National Council. Tensions rose between the Naga National Council and the Government of India after they tried to implement policies upon the Nagas which were fading their cultural identity because of which from within the Naga National Council – Nationalist Socialist Council of Nagaland (NSCN) was formed led by three prominent figures – Isak Chishi Suru, Thingaleng Muivah, (NSCN- IM) S.S. Khaplang (NSCN-K). Further, NSCN was divided into two parts (1)NSCN – IM (2)NSCN-K. In 1975, the Government of India signed the Shillong Accords with NSCN-IM bringing peace to the region. But the peace did not last long as it was during this time that NSCN-K led by S.S. Khaplang was formed separating themselves from NSCN-IM. The Government of India in response described NSCN-K as a Maoist breakaway group of the Naga National Council and labelled it as a terrorist group organization. Under the Unlawful Activities (Prevention) Act,1967(UAPA). Later, after the 2015 Manipur ambush during which a cross-border operation into Myanmar was carried out in response to the separatist's ambush on the military convoy in Chandel district in which 18 soldiers of the Indian Army lost their lives and many were found injured; in the cross-border operation, 15-20 separatists belonging to NSCN-K lost their life. Leading to which a new Naga political group named NSCN (reformation) was formed under the leadership of Wangtin Konyak. Indian Army under the belief of catching the insurgents of the Konyak terror group caused the death of civilians as claimed by the army.

Why do the people of Nagaland feel alienated from India?

Well, it is not only about Nagaland many other states i.e. the seven sisters namely Arunachal Pradesh, Meghalaya, Assam, Manipur, Nagaland, Tripura and Mizoram have a sense of separation from India. They are called the seven sisters because all the seven states are interdependent for food supply, or any other emergency. (Sikkim is the 8th state included in 2002). Because these seven sisters are joined through the central part by a narrow path called the 'Silly Guddi corridor' or the 'chicken neck corner'.

And the leftover parts arc being surrounded by China, Bhutan, and Bangladesh and adjacent to the seven sisters lies Myanmar where the 2015 operation was conducted. Thus giving the citizens of these states a more acquainted culture around our neighbouring countries and more chances of insurgencies. But geographical conditions aren't the only factors at which fingers can be pointed, we can't forget the discriminations faced by our north-eastern brothers and sisters during the pandemic when the speculations of Corona being a 'Chinese virus' were in talks leading to how people even from the capital had harassed them and made them feel alienated. Because of this incident, even the Chief Minister of Nagaland demanded the removal of the AFSPA Act of 1958 from the state, which under Section 7 provides for the protection of persons acting in good faith.

No prosecution, suit or legal proceeding shall be instituted

This act comes to the notice of people usually because of Jammu and Kashmir but we need to take notice of the fact that Nagaland was the first state where the act was implemented. The Act was formed keeping in mind the situation of Nagaland. I would like to conclude by bringing in the notice of my fellow readers about the discriminations faced by people from the north-eastern region of India because of their physical structure because " northeast India seamlessly fits(an) Indian's imagination of a Chinese person". Said a study commissioned by the Indian Council of Social Science Research (ICSSR) on racial discrimination and hate crimes against people from the northeast state. I hope this blog brings clarity to the thinking of my readers and helps us bring a new perspective towards Nagaland and other northeastern states.

CHAPTER THIRTEEN

GENDER STEREOTYPES: A CLICHÉ-RIDDEN NOTION

Author: Neha Kachhawaha, III year of B.B.A.,LL.B. from B.M. Law College

Neha Kachhawaha

Introduction

A very basic and overrated topic yet very tacit and unvoiced. We see everyplace around us in all field women are making their own spaces with all themselves. No matter what the situation is or if it's about their family, job, career, marriage women handle it all very smoothly with or without any external support. Even if there are many laws, statutes and rules made for the protection and equal rights of women in the society still when they are implemented in any way that if awoman becomes exceptionally successful in her profession society will often tell her that she is insanely goal oriented person. And these kinds of statements come from our society itself and also too often spoken by women who are either doing less in their careers and making judgements or who has fewer incentives and complaining for that.

There is no point of question that there has been a humongous change in the society and laws regarding gender stereotypes and gender gaps. So far there is also no point of question that the full gender equality has not been accomplished in many fields.There are many fields where women are still struggling as an individual for their equal rights and putting out their opinions. Gender Stereotypes is the one of the broader concepts which often includes subjects like gender roles, gender equality, gender discrimination, sexuality and many more.

Historical Background

Gender roles is one of the notions set by our societal expectations and norms from ancient times. Before independence there very few women who were able to stand out from the crowd, took stand for themselves, fought for their rights and set great examples in the society. Some of the stand outwomen, like Rani Lakshmibai, Queen of Jhansiwas one of theleading exemplars of theIndian Mutiny who fought against the Britishers in the battle field for an Independent India.Thereupon, Savitribai Phule together with her husband founded the first modern Indian Girl's School in Pune in 1848. She worked as an Indian social reformer, educationalist and beautiful poet. She also worked to abolish the discrimination and ill treatment of people based on their gender and caste[1].

In the wake of that when India finally got independent in 1947, it come up with its very own constitution which contributed towards the growth and success of the women in our society. Slowly and steadily women as a gender made their own spaces in every field today. Women like Mother Teresa, Indira Gandhi, Kalpana Chawla, Pratibha Patil, Kiran Bedi, Sania Mirza, Justice M. Fathima Beevi, Mary Kom and many more also shared their own stories with. Talking about one of the social activist and Padma Shri awardee currently who died on January 4th, 2022, Sindhutai Sapkal who was a social worker and was affectionately called as "Mai" nurtured over 1500 orphaned children. She has been honored with more than 700 awards till her death. Articulating another woman Falguni Nayar, a leading Indian businesswoman and billionaire who is founder and CEO of the beauty and lifestyle retail company Nykaa built to stand out from crowd.[2]

What are Gender Roles?

These are the societal expectations towards a particular gender to behave, act, conduct, dress in the way society has charged them with. Like for example a girl should be well dressed, emotional, polite, fair and on the other hand a man must be strong, masculine, and bold. A girl should always go for pink colors and boys for blue. A female must know how to do every household chore and male to be supremely intelligent and smart at their job and not in the kitchen. Even today if a maletries to take part in the household work or even while parenting, he is always been appreciated for even a smallest of his help. But the truth is that every single male should know that it his responsibility to do and know equally about his job and chore.

Outcome of Gender Stercotypes

This is stereotypical perception and a mindset towards a particular group of persons which can often cause unfair treatment and biasness towards that group. This is termed as Sexism. The gender stereotypes affect a lot to the mental, physical, emotional state of a person which can often lead to anxiety, depression, and other mental health problems.

It can be seen in different kinds like[3]:

1. Appearance: a female is expected to be thin and fair whereas a male should be tall, strong and handsome.
2. Job: a female must choose to be a nurse, teacher, orhousewife and a male should be an IIT or IIM pass out, an engineer or pilot.
3. Nature: a female should be polite, sweet and soft voiced, emotional whereas a male should be aggressive, self-confident and not a cry baby.

These overstated gender stereotypes do make relationship among the people hard and results in conflictbetween them. Until and unless we as an individual don't take stand for one self or others who are facing same problems in our surroundings this won't stop.

Measures to be Taken

What all steps you as a person can take:

•   Start it with yourself see if you too are making any kind of gender-based opinion and if yes then make a difference by changing and developing your thoughts by watching and reading right kind of information which is important for your growing mind.

- Try and put out your views and thoughts in front of your family, friends and relatives and peer groups to make them aware of these kinds of concepts by providing them right kind of information.
- Set yourself as an example in the society where people can get inspired by watching you doing great things and speaking out loud what is wrong and what is right.
- Give aid to those who ask for help and step-up for those of you think really needs to get helped.

These are just one of the ways where you can make a difference in the society. There can be many more ways to plant more stronger roots for our coming generations. And if we all work in homogeneity and harmony towards this kind of issue there can be much greater difference in patriarchal nation and world as whole.

Conclusion

Coming to an end of this topic one can definitely say that Gender Stereotypes and Gender Roles is one of the concerning subjects presently. If these differences and gaps are not covered now then it will become problem for our future generation. Treating every group of people and community whether its male, female or any person from LGBTQ community is the most essential part of a developing nation.

Author's Biography

My name is Neha Kachhawaha.I'm pursuing my BB. A LL.B course from B.M. Law College, Jodhpur. I'm exploring different fields in law and writing is one of them and my most liked. As I'm an introvert writing makes me feel like I can share my thoughts and perspective with the world. And as it is well said by Anne Frank " I can shake off everything as I write; my sorrow disappear, my courage is reborn."

SHOULD AN INVENTOR APPLY FOR THE PATENT WITHOUT PROFESSIONAL ASSISTANCE IN INDIA

Author: Shashank Singh Rathor, II year of B.A.,LL.B. from Ideal Institute of Management & Technology and School of Law, Affiliated to G.G.S.I.P.U. , Delhi

Shashank Singh Rathor

Introduction

As India is on its way to becoming one of the innovation hubs in Asia, patent filing is getting momentum in the country. The distinct initiatives by the Indian government to encourage innovators and startups are also playing a key role in the increasing rate of filing patents in the nation. In 2020 itself 24 thousand industrial patents were granted in India. It clearly shows that the innovators and startups are now pretty much keen on getting their innovation patented, safeguarding them from any kind of infringement and potential market competitors, and further enjoying monopolistic and exclusive business gains. Further, it has led to an elevation in awareness of patent filing.

It could not be neglected that filing a patent is an extensive as well as an expensive process in India. Generally, while filling a patent, just the statutory filing fees (official fee) and professional fees are disclosed. However, after the due process of filing the patent, there are certain other fees that are to be paid to the Indian Patent Office (IPO), and after paying this much if I will say that this amount is not something that is only to be paid for filing a patent, what will be your reaction? This article will answer, whether the inventor should approach professional help for filing the patent or not.

Who can apply for a patent in India

Section 6 of The Patent Act, 1970 talks about, who is entitled to make an application for a patent? As per the provision provided under Section 6 of the act, anyone who is the first and true inventor of the invention can apply for the patent of his/her invention. However, as per the provision in Section 6, such a right of filing the application can be transferred to the assignee of the first and true inventor of the invention. In such circumstances, the application has to be accompanied by proof of right to make an application with the declaration that the person who is claiming is the first and true inventor of the invention. Last but not least, the patent application can also be filed by the legal representative of any deceased person who was entitled to such a patent before his death.

Why you might apply for a patent without an attorney

In India filling a patent with the help of a professional or attorney will cost you approximately INR 50,000-INR 70,000 which will account for 75 to 95% of the total fee. Probably, you might have listened about the term, "prosecute" in other contexts, when it comes to patents; the prosecution is only a process of guiding a patent application through the Indian Patent Office (IPO). Of course, it is not mandatory to hire a professional or a patent law firm for the filling process, Inventors can undertake the whole patent process by themselves and it must not be neglected that without proper corporate or institutional funding, it's barely possible for many new inventors, students, and individuals to hire a legal representative for themselves.

Fortunately in India, there is no rule that it's mandatory to involve a patent attorney for filing the patent application. If the inventor is capable of filling the application on his own and has that much time and willingness to learn the process, then he may file his patent application on his own.

While deciding whether or not to work with a patent lawyer, the inventor should always consider the following points :

- Whether you have that much time to conduct your research and follow through with the application process.
- The level of complexity of your invention. The more complicated and advanced your invention and its technology are, the more likely you will need an attorney.
- What are the possibilities that others will challenge your invention? If your invention is pretty much similar to the other's invention or it is in a competitive field, then in such a situation, you may need an attorney to draft a really strong patent that will stand up to all the legal challenges.

Some of the reasons, which might influence the inventors to proceed with the patenting process on their own

Now, moving on to the pinpoint of the whole issue, what are the possible reasons that make the inventors proceed with the patenting process on their own? First thing first, the inventor should have to draft the strong patent application before filing it, and if he doesn't have any idea about drafting the patent application then legal assistance comes into the picture which can surely charge a hefty amount of money for drafting. In India, filing the patent might cost the inventor in lacs or it also depends on the selection of the Patent Consultant or law firm for his work. If someone goes to the law firm, they charge so much that most individuals drop the idea, and on the other hand, if someone goes to the less experienced patent agent who lacks the skills of drafting a good patent application then the amount charged by them might be very little but cannot be trusted for reliable work.

Some of the probable causes are mentioned below, which might influence the inventors to proceed with the patenting process on their own:

- Financial constraints
- It can also be possible that the inventor might have thought that, since he is the inventor, he is the best person to describe his invention and that's why professional help is not required.
- An inventor who has previously prepared public disclosures and has some experience of preparing it might feel that preparing a patent specification is a similar task, that he can perform on his own.
- Most probably the inventor might be having thought, that filing for a patent is just an administrative process and can be done by filling up and submitting the form.

Advantages

- An inventor may save thousands of rupees if he files his application without an attorney.
- Moreover, he may qualify for free or low-cost resources to assist with the patent application process.

Disadvantages

- The inventor will have to do exhaustive research, including prior art searches, before filing.
- It will mostly take hundreds of hours of your own time for filing a patent application without legal help.
- You will be required to stay on top of and meet the many important requirements and deadlines of the application process.
- Further, drafting a strong application requires excellent writing skills.

Can you get a strong patent without legal assistance

- A stronger patent can provide you with a stronger claim on your invention, so it must be drafted with utmost care. A stronger patent always presents well-written claims, displays usefulness, distinguishes a new invention from the prior art, and foremost thing can anticipate legal challenges.

- Further, the well-grounded claims are what truly strengthen a patent. This is often the most significant task for an attorney, as the claims elucidate your invention in a way that will be used to determine if someone is infringing your patent.
- While drafting the patent, the most complicated part is to predict the legal challenges on your own; this is such a sensitive part of the filing process that even patent agents cannot provide the relevant information, as this would be considered legal advice.
- To save the cost, you may try to identify vulnerabilities on your own. However, the amount of risk will always revolve around the nature of your invention. What type of invention is it? Is it innovative enough in the extremely competitive field? Are there similar inventions in the market?

These are some of the few challenges the inventor might face if he will try to draft it on his own but if he is really keen to do that and there isn't any option left to him. Then, a thorough patent search can assist him in finding out the other patent holders who might challenge him.

Conclusion

Patents can give great value and increased returns to inventors and companies on the investment made in evolving new technology. Patenting process needs to be done with a well-planned strategy that aligns business interests to implement the technology with a wide range of options in the search for how, where, and when to patent. It must be understood that a patent specification is the only document that protects the invention, and hence, it should be drafted with the utmost care and by the best person for this job. It is highly recommended that the inventors should not try to do this job if they are not qualified for doing this because ultimately it can affect their patent rights. They may try to do so if they have certain skills that are required for filing patents and are willing to do at their own risk.

VIRTUAL COURTS & ACCESS TO JUSTICE – A STEP FORWARD FOR INDIAN JUDICIARY?

Author: Komal Agrawal, III year of B.A.,LL.B. from KIIT Law School, KIIT University, Bhubaneswar

Komal Agrawal

Abstract

The concept of virtual court has been central to the legal world & has influenced the Indian Courts & judicial system enormously amidst the Covid-19 pandemic. In fact, in the present scenario, any aggrieved person can access justice around every corner of the country. Virtual courts can be defined as the court system where all documents & proceedings related to the ongoing case can be recorded electronically & the arguments can be heard via video conferencing. When the nationwide lockdown was ordered, it was evidently not possible for the courts to be effective & continue with the physical submissions & hearings. But in any way, justice was to be delivered because "Justice delayed is Justice denied". The pandemic posed a huge threat to the Indian judiciary system initially. All courts were ceased from operating in addition to the heavy backlog of cases crippling Indian judiciary. Therefore, the virtual court concept was adopted, where subsequently, the Supreme Court (SC) strongly provided shield to its 'virtual courts framework', and observed that the institutional prerequisite was to guarantee the 'administration of justice', which shall not disintegrate despite the pandemic. This article focuses on the opportunities available to & challenges being faced by the virtual courts in India.

Courts - A service or a Place?

After a transition to the virtual courts, people started debating over whether the courts are a service or a place. If courts are to be taken as a service then the Indian judiciary system can deliver justice by continuing with the digital realm while if the same are to be taken as a place then proceedings through virtual realm do not seem to be a constructive idea in long run.

But the situation worsened when some of the significant legislations like Civil procedure Code (CPC), Code of Criminal Procedure (CrPC) and General Clauses Act, 1897 does not define the "Court". But the legal acronyms of the Legislative Department defines "Court" as a place where justice is administered while Black's legal glossary defines Court as a governmental body that consists of judges for the settlement of disputes. Though the courts have different meanings, they point towards two similar components that clarifies our question of whether courts are a service or a place; firstly courts are the government bodies consisting of more judges and secondly the purpose of establishment of courts is to deliver justice.

Henceforth, a court showcases more of a service characteristic than that of a place. The concept of virtual courts is not a new phenomenon but just that it has been more highlighted owing to the global pandemic. So, virtual courts have become a necessity to deliver justice as a service as courts do not need a place to provide justice.

Comment

According to the 103rd Report of the Rajya Sabha on Functioning of Virtual Courts/Court Proceedings via Video Conferencing, several opportunities & challenges were announced while accepting the new concept of virtual courts.[1]The report was presented by the Department-related Parliamentary Standing Committee On Personnel, Public Grievances, Law And Justice.

It is a matter of fact that no other system of courts can ever replace physical courts because physical courts administers justice on a fundamental theory of open court laid down in the Indian Constitution. The President of the Supreme Court Bar Association was of the view that the virtual proceedings by the Supreme Court was nowhere near up to the mark & was extremely dis satisfactory.

The virtual court system created a situation of digital divide in the use of digital platform by making justice beyond the reach for the bulk of the population. It was observed that most of the advocates & legal professionals residing in rural areas lacked proper network connectivity and outworn audio-video equipment which is an essential requirement to participate in the virtual hearing of the cases.

The Committee notified that most advocates do not possess the required digital knowledge of the technology and owing to their technological incompetence, they showed a major concern that this might put them in an unadvantageous position over those advocates & professionals who have adequate digital literacy & no network connectivity issues.

Besides technological issues, there are significant issues like cyber security & data breach in India. The committee informed that the virtual courts can lead to exposing privacy & revealing the confidential information. There ain't any law that guarantees data security as Indian Courts gets aid from apps like Cisco, Vidya which stresses a risk towards privacy of data.

There will also be very high chances of presenting false testimony of witnesses & malicious evidence to dislocate the facts of the case. The testimony of witnesses allows the court to investigate the details relevant to the case & examine the testimonies provided by witnesses along with their acts & gestures which enables the lawyers to detect the true facts. In virtual medium it is easier for the parties to mislead the courts by testifying falsely & presenting false evidences.

The chief advantage of virtual court system is that it is easily accessible, affordable with minimal or zero cost of need for travel. It is both cost saving & time saving as hearing takes place at intervals & there's no need for lawyers to assemble in a single venue before hours. There are various cases where hearing is not necessary & such cases can be disposed off by cutting down unnecessary costs & time. So, Virtual courts can also help in dealing with the problem of backlog of cases by disposing the cases according to the specific needs. The virtual courts system is more flexible as lawyers & advocates can conveniently present arguments for more than one case a day without any need to travel. They can be present in the hearing even from their place of work. Therefore, justice can be delivered faster with resources in virtual court system.

Post Pandemic Future of Virtual Courts

After discussing various challenges & opportunities in virtual court system, it is quite evident that virtual court system is the need of the Indian judiciary to administer justice even in the wake of Covid-19. But the question is whether virtual court system is a permanent substitute of physical courts ? Justice D.Y. Chandrachud said that in the near future, virtual courts are not going to replace physical courts & that the scope of virtual courts shall be extended & should be more standardized all over the nation. Also, the legal & professional ethics are to be applied while the court proceedings. In no case, the discipline & integrity of the court should be compromised.

The Supreme Court can also opt for a mixture of both virtual court & physical court system. It could allow the courts to squeeze more benefits of the best of both system - saving costs and time, flexibility in addition to maintenance of fairness & ensuring justice and prove advantageous to both the public & Indian Judiciary.

Conclusion

The Indian Constitution incorporated the doctrine of Rule of Law to ensure access to justice by every citizen. Justice, shall in no circumstance, be denied to the general public. To survive in this global pandemic & allow the courts to function, a new system of virtual court hearing was developed. Undoubtedly, many scholars and legal professionals have extended their support to encourage & accept the virtual court system and to continue eventually after this pandemic ends. After discussing both challenges & opportunities it would not be unfair to say that the opportunities outcasted by virtual framework of hearing cases supersede the challenges & could be made a better service by bringing required changes.

However, this digital court hearing framework must be kept temporary & be limited to the current pandemic. The open courtrooms for administering justice cannot be substituted by the digital court hearing. The virtual courts cannot become a norm as they have to perform their functions physically after the normalization of the situation. Accepting virtual court as a norm would would manifest that the building in which we sit & deliver justice should be closed down. Though virtual court allows the litigants to seek justice at a very minimal cost but that would go against the basic principle embodied in Indian Constitution & undermine the fundamental doctrine of Rule of Law. It would also go against the provisions enlisted in Indian Penal Code (IPC) and Code of Criminal Procedure (CrPC) which promotes open courts delivering open justice. The 18th century English Philosopher Jeremy Bentham quoted, "The courts shall be open for the public to enhance public confidence in the justice delivery system". Therefore, virtual courts are to me made limited only to the length of the ongoing crisis in view of the administration of justice, integrity & majesty of open court hearings.

CHAPTER SIXTEEN

ECONOMIC RESERVATION

Author: Saranya Adhikari, V year of B.B.A.,LL.B. from Uttaranchal University, Law College Dehradun

Introduction

"Not every DNA carries wealth and reconnaissance; not everyone with a surname needs upliftment. It's time to stop being greedy and help the needy, else cut the lie of mentioning the right to equality."

Reservation summons in common terms to an act of reserving keeping back or restrain the seats which are reserved in public sector units, union and state civil services for members of economically backwards class, tribes and community reservation is governed by many laws such as constitutional laws, statutory laws and local rules and regulations. The concept of reservation was introduced by B.R Ambedkar. The inspection of the reservation system came after India got independence because before a quota system favoring caste and other fraternity existed.

Meaning

Economic means the economic principle to analyze the various laws made for the protection of society at large. Economic reservation means securing justice, liberty, equality, fraternities to its citizens. Economic reservation says that 10% of reservation should be given to economically backward classes in the society.

Dr. Ambedkar wrote that "Men love property more than liberty". This Bill was made for the betterment of the societies and lower communities it was amendedso that the backward classes could get equal chance in the society to prove themselves because upper classes never wanted to grow and to be equal and also that they could earn theirlivelihood as they were unaware of the facilities and they have low income. A recent example of Kerala is that one Schedule Caste person stole rice and he was starved to death. It gives a life stability as many people die of hunger so they are the ones who actually needs to get equal respect and jobs in the society because in earlier times the lower caste used to clean toilets of upper class and they were not allowed to sit beside them and hence this has still been escorted in some of the urban areas.

Historical Background

Economic reservation means that 10% of reservation should be given to the economic backward classes The Economic Reservation bill was amended by the Constitution 103rd Amendment act 2019 which amended article 15 and 16 and clause 6 has been added in this which say that the 10% of post in each category like in government jobs and educational institutions should be given to economic backward classes other than the class mentioned in clause 4 and 5. The act was executed on 14 January 2019 it was passed by the Rajya Sabha on January 9 2019 with the support of 165 members and in Lok Sabha by the two-third majority with 323 members passed in favor of amending the bill.

Objective

The public acceptance on the reservation of the bill was that the bill will give them an equal opportunity and equal protection to all the citizens and that there will not be solely discriminated on the grounds of religion, caste, sex, and place of birth. The bill will give them an equalopportunity to improvethe status of historically oppressedgroups like schedule castes, and other backward class. They said that the amendment aims to fulfillthe commitments of the directive principals of the state policy under article 46 which promotes for the economic interests and educational interest in the weaker sections of the society.

The condition before the amendment of the act was that quota system existed demands of various forms of discrimination were made people were not given equal opportunity as they were economically weak they needed financial support as well as reservation to corroborate fair access to education as well as employment The economic status of the person changethey were infested with corruption and used to make fake certificate from the authorities. The upper classes of group were given power to monopolies state and the backward classes used to feel inferior or sometimes even verified. Existing reservation policies were highly unpopular and common caste discrimination in India was the practice of untouchability.

Benefit

The benefit which enjoyed afterthe amendment of the act was that people could take advantage of 10% of reservation system on the educational institutions and public employment. Several committees were set up where quantifiable data was assemblage highlighting the need for having reservation

The expression of creamy layer is for highly cultivated people who are economically socially, educationally weak. It was first introduced by the Sattanathan commission in 1971. He said that the creamy layer which is used for the OBC, scheduled caste, and schedule tribes should eliminate the reservations quota of civil posts. The concept of creamy layer says that the backward classes should be restricted to initial appointments not on extending to promotions.

In the case of Indra Sawhney v. Union of India[1] In this the concept of qualitative exclusion such as "creamy layer" was introduced. It was said that the concept of creamy layer should be excluded and it provides reservation to the extent of only 10% to the other category and the general category for the in society.

The people entitled for benefit are

The person who is entitled for the benefit of reservation are the poor segments classes and upper caste which include Hindus and as well other religion in Hinduism it is proposed to Brahmins, Rajput, Jaat, Marathas ,Bhumihars, Vaishya ,along with Patidar, Gujjar depending upon the caste group. The criteria for reservation were that it should only be implemented to those backward people who has annual income less than 8 lakhs, or those people who have less than 5 acres of land, or less than 1,000 square feet in town. The S.C of India ruled in 1992 that reservation could not exceeds more than 50% and in those in which it exceed more than 50% they are the state which are under litigation of Supreme court,for example, in state of Tamil Nadu, there are 87% of the population out of which reservation stands only 69%. Reservation SC, ST, and OBC but they are also made for the women'sand transgender so they can get equal scope. The framers of the constitution believed that caste system of SCs and the STs were decline and historically oppressed in an Indian Society because they did not have equal opportunities.

Challenge

The challenge of the amendment of the economicreservation was that petition was filed in the Supreme Court by non – government organization named Youth of Equality on the ground that the amendment violates the basic structure of the constitution as article 14 of the constitution talks about the right of equality and moreover the amendment provides for a 10% economic reservation over and above the existing reservation. Another challenge was on the basis of constitutionally of the amendment is arbitrariness when the upper caste has already got the interest of reservation they shall not be allowed to use the benefit of reservation again.

Judicial Pronouncement

The Judicial pronouncement was making reservation for the backward classes. In case of State of Madras v. Champakam Dorairajan[2]and Another in this case Supreme Court first time bestow with the issue of reservation. it was said that reservation shall only be 50%, This specification first raised in the case of M.R Balaji v. State of Mysore [3] It was held in this case that only 50% reservation shall be given the reservation above 50% shall implicit dominance over article 16(1). In case of State of Kerala v. N.M Thomas[4] the S.C held that the "weaker sections "mentioned in article (46) does not only include backward classes but also those categories comparable economically and educationally, to schedule caste and schedule tribes. In case of Ashoka Kumar Thakur v. Union of India [5] in this case it was held that sustaining constitutionally validity of Central Educations Institutions Reservation in admission act in 2006 it cannot only be based on caste other parameters such as backwardclass is also included in this category. In case of Chitralekha v. State of Mysore[6]in this case it was held that in many groups classes and caste are not pertinent for example, agriculture labourers, street- hawkers, rickshaw puller and etc. because they will qualify as being designated as backward class The constitutional challenge was on the basis of the basic structure doctrine it was said that only 50% reservation should be given to the backward classes. In the case of I.C Golaknath v State of Punjab[7] in this case it was held by Supreme Court of India that the provisions of the fundamental right can be amended by passing a constitutional amendment act as per the requirement of article 368 but latter on it was overruled and it was held that the fundamental right contorted in part III of the constitution would be preclude from the ambit of amendment conferred in 368. In the case of Kesavananda Bharti v State of Kerala[8]this case overruled the judgment made in Golaknath and it said that the same objective specified in the preamble of the constitution cannot be amended in the exercise of power conferred in article 368. The Parliament cannot use its amending competence to damage, destroy abrogate, change, emasculate the basic structure of constitution.

Conclusion

The positive effectof the reservation is that it gives an opportunity to the poor backward classes to prove themselves in the society also people living in India Pakistan border in Jammu and Kashmir will get the benefit of the reservation. People can also avail benefit of reservation in promotion, admission in different professional courses, and in direct recruitment. People from the backward sectionscan achieve higherpost and servicesin the public sector. The reservation will help them to encourage and fight back for their justice they will also be brought up to the same level and this process will forward them in being rich.

The negative impact of the reservation is that there is a discrimination between the upper classes and lower classes a sections of Indians will never be allowed to grow it will take them more time to reach the level of education. The poor caste will get the privilege through the caste system and they will hog the reserved scats for example there are students who have SC, ST, and OBC but they are also made for the women's and transgender so they can get equal scope. The framers of the constitution believed that caste system of SCs and the STs were decline and historically oppressed in an Indian Society because they did not have equal opportunities.

CHAPTER SEVENTEEN

THE PHILOSPHY OF SUICIDE: WHAT IS JUSTICE?

Author: Rishi Kumar Singh, I year of B.A.,LL.B. from Lloyd Law College, Uttar Pradesh

Rishi Kumar Singh

Suicide, an act of taking one's own life usually by hanging, poisoning by pesticides, drowning, jumping from great height, drug overdose, shooting and by using firearms are again on mutiny. This is the one of the biggest stumbling block of progress in the running 21st century. It is perceived in the present era most often usually in all age group but surprisingly in young teens also who entered in the dawn of the life. In this article I will give you glimpse of history of suicide, how it evolved and various such aspects related to it.

Why Suicide rate jumped with modernization?

Paradoxically, the data on suicide astounds everyone. Especially comparing it to rural and undeveloped places, it is found to be greater in percentage in urban and developed areas. In wealthy countries, it is substantially greater than in undeveloped countries. Suicide rates are increasing with the passage of time. The question of why surfaces once more.

The rationale is straightforward. Previously, civilization was based on myth. The legends of GODS and DEMONS were held in high regard. Any misfortune that befell on somebody was supposed to be a Demon's curse, or that God was assembling his puppet for the impending future hitch. It was simply assumed that God had done this to them and people believed that no individual played a role in their unfortunate fate. However, as time passed, a faith in science and scientific evidence gained. Every disaster has a purpose, people have discovered. Individualism and hard effort become profoundly ingrained in culture.

People realized that if you work hard you will succeed or you will lag behind. This gave rise to stiff competition. To the immature youthful mind, competition gave rise to bad phrases like stress, worry, sadness, split personality disorder, and eventually agonizing agony. Finally, actions such as suicide were taken.

Suicide Composition Tree

NCRB (The National Crime Records Bureau) is a government body in India tasked with gathering and analyzing crime statistics as mandated by the Indian Penal Code (IPC) and Special and Local Laws (SLL). It has given data that the highest rate of suicide is seen in daily wage earner followed by housewife, other person, self employed person, unemployed person, professional and salaried person, student, person engaged in farming sector and finally retired person. Maharashtra bagged the unfortunate top list. The main reason is poverty followed by unemployment, drug abuse, family problem and educational overload. A suicide is committed in every 4 min in our country. 381 suicides is committed every day. If we multiply 381 to 365 it will take calculator to get the result. Males commit suicide 4 times more than female. The usually preferred mode of suicide was hanging followed by self poisoning. Now the question arises does education plays any role in preventing suicide? The answer is that only 3.7% suicide rate is seen in graduated young Indian compared to other lower level of educated persons, so yes education obstructs the growing rate of suicide.

Right to Die is Fundamental Right or Not ?

In Maruti Shipati Dubal Vs State of Maharastra, 1987 the court threw light that Right to live as recognized by Article 21 will also include a right not to live or not to be forced to live. To put it positively it would include a right to die or to terminate one's life. Also, Section 309 of IPC prescribes the same punishment to all individual irrespective the different set of circumstances under which suicide attempt is made. The Court said that these two laws are contradictor to each other. But Section 309 being arbitrary is ultra virus of Article 14 of Indian Constitution.

In Chenna Jagadeshwar and ANR. Vs The State of Andra Pradesh, the Court found that Section 309 is valid and does not offend the Article 19 and Article 21 of the Indian Constitution. Now the question came before The Apex Court.

In P.Rathinam Vs Union of India AIR 1994 the court explored that Section 309 violates Article 21 and so, it is void since Section 309 of Indian Penal Code deserved to be effaced from the statue book to humanize our Indian Penal Laws. It is cruel and an irrational provision and it may result in punishing a person again i.e. doubly who has suffered agony and would be undergoing ignominy because of his failure to commit suicide. Finally in Gain Kaur Vs State of Punjab AIR 1996 the Apex Court overruled the previous judgments verdicting that Section 306 and Section 309 are independent provisions. The Court said that suicide is unnatural termination of one's own life so the Section 309 is valid.

A Special Case : EUTHANASIA

Euthanasia is a painless killing of a patient suffering from an incurable and painful disease or an irreversible coma. This practice is legal as well as illegal in many countries of the world.

In Gian Kaur Vs The State of Punjab, AIR 1996 the court said that a dying person who is terminally ill or in a persistent vegetative state may be permitted to terminate his or her own life. Right to not live can be covered under such injunctions. But The Apex Court said that the euthanasia should be made lawful only through legislation. In Aruna Ramchandra Shangaug Vs Union of India 2011 the court said that the passive euthanasia should be permitted in our country in certain circumstances , and disagreed ....that it should never be permitted.

Is Suicide Really Justified?

Young person below the age of 25 even commits suicide. We should think that what psychological pressure they were going through that they feel so trapped that they decide to give full stop to their life. Suicide is indeed is not a pleasurable thing. The process to take decision to commit suicide is so horrible that we cannot imagine.

CHAPTER EIGHTEEN

UNTOUCHABILITY AND ARTICLE 17: A HISTORICAL ANALYSIS

Author: Sakshi Soni, III year of B.A.,LL.B.(Hons.) from School of Law, NMIMS Indore

INTRODUCTION

"The incorporation of Article 17 into the Constitution is symbolic of valuing the centuries' old struggle of social reformers and revolutionaries. It is a move by the Constitution makers to find catharsis in the face of historic horrors. It is an attempt to make reparations to those, whose identity was subjugated by the society."[1]

-Justice D.Y. Chandrachud

Untouchability, an ancient form of discrimination based upon caste, is a complex and pervasive problem within India, although its practice is not limited to India alone.[2] The discrimination is so inhumane that it made the Dalits to believe that they are responsible for their own exclusion and suffering, internalizing the beliefs that they perpetuate the practice untouchability. The practice of untouchability has marginalised, terrorized and relegated a sector of Indian society to a life larked by the violence, humiliation and indignity.[3] The biggest paradox of the world's largest democracy is that a particular section of society i.e. dalits are still fighting for their equal rights. The practice of untouchability and caste discrimination remains a stark contrast to the idea of India. Untouchability a "hidden apartheid" remains an extremely sensitive issue within country which never fully defines, never fully explored and thus, never fully understood. Since 2001, with the United Nations World Conference against Racism held in Durban, South Africa the caste- based discrimination and untouchability had become an extremely sensitizing issue for the world. United Nations has consistently raised awareness on every kind of human right violation. Article 1 of the Declaration of Human Rights adopted by the U.N.O. declares that "All the human beings are born free and in equal dignity and rights, they are endowed with reason and conscience and should act towards one another in a spirit of brotherhood".

Despite the increasing domestic and international concern over untouchability, a constitutional prohibition against it, laws that implement this constitutional prohibition and international human rights watch, the life of many Dalits seems unchanged. The discriminatory regime of untouchability remains unshakable.

From the time immemorial, Untouchables have been deprived even of their basic human rights. Dr Ambedkar the Chief Architect of the Indian Constitution was elected as chairman of the Drafting Committee for preparing a draft Constitution of India on August 30, 1947. In his closing speech on the Draft constitution delivered on November 25, 1949 he said: "What we must do is not to be attained with mere political democracy; we must make our political democracy a social democracy as well. Political Democracy cannot last unless there lies on the basis of it as social democracy." Further in his speech he said "Social democracy means a way of life which recognizes liberty, equality and fraternity as principles of life." They are not separate items in a trinity but they form union of trinity. To diverse one from the other is to defeat the very purpose of democracy. Without equality, liberty would produce the supremacy of the few over the many. Equality without liberty would kill individual initiative. Without fraternity, liberty and equality could not become a natural course of things." The disabilities to which Dalits were subjected have been outlawed and subjecting them to those disabilities would be violative of the Part III and IV of the Constitution.[4]The main thrust of Article 17 is to liberate the society from blind and ritualistic adherence and traditional beliefs. It seeks to establish a new and ideal society.

<u>DEFINITIONAL ASPECT: 'UNTOUCHABILITY'</u>

Article 17. Abolition of Untouchability: - "Untouchability" is abolished and its practice in any form is forbidden. The enforcement of any disability arising out of "Untouchability" shall be an offence punishable in accordance with law.The word 'Untouchability' has not been defined in this article. Similar is the case with the Protection of Civil Rights Act, 1955, in which 'Untouchability' is nowhere defined. However, Mahatma Gandhi in 'My

Philosophy of Life' stated that 'untouchability means pollution by the touch of certain persons by reasons of their birth in a particular state of family. It is a phenomenon peculiar to Hinduism and has got no warrant in reasons or sastras."[5]According to Dr Ambedkar, "The untouchability is the notion of defilement, pollution, contamination and the ways and means of getting rid of that defilement. It is a permanent hereditary stain which nothing can cleanse."[6]

<u>ORIGIN OF UNTOUCHABLES</u>

When discussing the practice of untouchability, it is very important to trace its origin and how the stigma of being 'untouchable' get attached with a particular section of the society. Based on Hindu beliefs, Principle of Varna-Ashrama-Dharmastructured the Indian society into four castes called Brahmans, Kshatriya, Vaisyas, and Shudras and one additional caste called the Untouchable. The principle of Chaturvarna is first mentioned and elaborated in the Purusha Sukta, the tenth and last Hymn of the Rig Veda. The glimpses of this concept can also be seen in the Atharva Veda and the Yajur Veda. According to the Purusha Sukta, when the God Prajapati created the world, he divided Purusha, a comic man who is immortal and diffused everywhere over things and universe, into many parts and from each part, a category of people was produced.[7] As Ambedkar also stated, "The Brahmans were his mouth; the Rajanya were his arms; the being called the Vaisyas were his thighs; and the Shudras sprang from his feet."[8]Brahmans were recognized as the superioramong all castes, the Kshatriyas were placed next in the hierarchy, the Vaisyas lower than the Kshatriyas, and the Shudras were given lowest place. This hierarchy of castes had been supported and propagated by the sutra writers and finally laid down in the Law of Manu. Manusmriti, the main architect of the Hindu society, confirmed the divine injunction of what had been set out in the Purusha Sukta and enunciated the duties of each caste specifically[9], as follows:

- For the Brahmins, he mentioned teaching, study, sacrifices and sacrificing (as priests) for others, also giving and receiving gifts.
- For the Kshatriyas, he ordered defence of the people, sacrifice, study and absence of attachment to object of sense.
- Tending of cattle, giving (alms, sacrifice, study, trade and agriculture) for Vaishyas.

- Only one duty was assigned to Shudras, serve to those classes without grudging.

On the basis of origin and by particular sacrament, these four castes are distinguished. The first three castes i.e. Brahmans, Kshatriya and Vaishya are called Dvija, twice born whereas the last caste, the Shudras does not the sacraments, so they are non- Dvija or once- born. The nature of caste system is vey rigid, as it based on birth and unalterable. The caste system established the superiority of Brahmans and provided them the title of 'God on earth'. Shudras were given the lowest position in this social hierarchy. Hindu civilization has further produced a fifth varna or panchama called the Untouchables who are excluded from the caste system and excluded from the society whose touch are enough to cause impurity. Both Shudras and Untouchables belong to non- Dvija. The only distinction marked between the Shudras and Untouchables is that, Shudras are still considered as human beings whereas untouchables are not even recognized as humans and receive sub- human status. The term Untouchable is essentially derived from the notions of defilement, pollution, and contamination.[10]

Jawahar Lal Nehru in Discovery of India, stated that Indian social structure had degraded a mass of human beings and given them no opportunities to get out of that condition- educationally, culturally and economically.[11]

STRUGGLE FOR IDENTITY

"Raidas ek boond saun, tabhi machau vichaar,

Moorakh hain jo karat hai, baran- abaran vichar."

(Ravidas says that it is foolish to know about caste of a person, as human being is a small unit created by the God. He compares him with a small drop.)[12]

Saints of medieval period of Indian history are known for cultural protest. The saints like Ravidas, Kabir, Malukdas and Navaldas raised their voices against slavery, untouchability, exploitation, caste system, blind faiths, idolatry and prohibition of entry of dalits in public places. The Untouchables referred as one of the Depressed Classes by the Indian government from the middle of 19th century. In 1935, the Government of India Act introduced the term "Scheduled Castes" which incorporated the untouchables in the scheduled (list) of castes which provided for reserved scats throughout the British Administered provinces.[13] Ambedkar also wanted to give the untouchables a nomenclature of the Avarna or

'Protestant Hindus'.[14] However, it is evident that he often used ' Scheduled Castes' in writing and oral statements like in Simon Commission 1928, Round Table Conferences of 1930- 1932 and in many more summits. More, often than not, he preferred to address them as the Untouchables to remind them of their plight as dehumanised people.[15]

Gandhi gave another dimension of their identities. He called them 'Harijans' or 'Children of God' however many studies revels that this term is not accepted by the people of this section because Mahatma Gandhi advocated the caste system. In addition, they did not like the word 'Harijan' because it is also used to refer to the fatherless children of temple prostitutes.[16] Untouchables started to address themselves Dalits. The term Dalit is rooted in Marathi language which means 'suppressed and exploited people.' Dr Ambedkar also used this to represent the Untouchables. They were also called as Pariahs or outcastes who had been excluded by the Caste Hindus from the Varna System.

However, Dalit gained greater recognition with the establishment of the Dalit Panther Political Party founded by Namdev Dhasal, J.V Pawar and others in April 1972 in Mumbai. Dalit Panthers were ideologically aligned with the Black Panthers Party, a social organisation fighting against racism in United States. They gained prominence during the 70's and 80's after the Republican Party founded by Dr B.R. Ambedkar split into multiple factions.[17] In 1984, with the emergence of the Bahujan Samaj Party (BSP), the more inclusive term Bahujana came to refer the Scheduled Castes, Scheduled Tribes and the other Backward Castes to the Untouchables.[18] The Untouchables were also addressed by many other names such as Dasa, Dasyu, Chandala, Panchama and Adisudra. Despites the various names and labels given to Untouchables, their lives remain still oppressed, deprived and disabled.

<u>CONSTITUTIONAL RIGHT AND CONSTITUTIONAL VISION: ARTICLE 17</u>

"Untouchability" is abolished and its practice in any form is forbidden. The enforcement of any disability arising out of "Untouchability" shall be an offence punishable in accordance with law.

-Article 17, Constitution of India

Article 17 firstly makes a declaration for the abolition of untouchability and prohibits its practice in any form.

Secondly, it declares that the enforcement of any disability arising out of untouchability is to be an offence punishable in accordance with the law.

This part of the article should be read with Article 35 of the Constitution which empowers the Parliament to make appropriate laws punishing as offence every act of individuals or groups which tantamount to applying disability arising out of untouchability.

The main thrust of Article 17 is to liberate the society from blind and ritualistic adherence and traditional beliefs. It seeks to establish a new and ideal society. The disabilities to which Dalits were subjected, have been outlawed and subjecting them to those disabilities would be violative of the Part III and IV of the Constitution.[19]

However, the term "Untouchability" is nowhere defined. Article 17 of the Constitution is on the lines of the provisions of Article 2 of the Universal Declaration of Human Rights. It is a very important and significant provision from the point of view of equality before law.[20] It guarantees social justice and dignity of man, the twin privileges which were denied to a vast section of the Indian society for centuries together.[21] According to Dr Durga Das Basu[22] Article 17 is one of the few anomalous provisions included in Part III of our Constitution. The reasons cited by him are:

1. Firstly, Untouchability arises out of the conduct of private individual and can hardly be committed by the State. Article 17 is practically levelled against private conduct and has little place in public law. Of course, it envisages a law to implement and the Article to be made by the Parliament [Art. 35 (a) (ii)] but that is only enabling provision.[23] The only justification for its inclusion in Part III as against State action may be that any law made before the Constitution which might be inconsistent with the abolition of untouchability would be void under Art. 13 (1).[24]

2. Secondly, Article 17 does not establish any right in favour of the person against whom untouchability have been practised but merely, forbids an action on the part of the wrongdoer and prescribes namely that he will be punishable according to a law to be made by Parliament.[25]

In Deverajia v Padmanna[26], hon'ble court observed that untouchability refers to the social disabilities historically imposed on certain classes of the people by reason of their birth in certain castes and would not include an instigation of social boycott by reason of the conduct of certain persons. Therefore, the term "untouchability" under Article 17 has been used under the inverted comas because the subject matter of Article 17 is not untouchability in its literal or grammatical sense, but the practice as it had developed historically in this country and that the word "untouchability" is used in that sense in this Article.[27]

Article 17 is a prospective legislation and laws in force in the state before the commencement of the constitution are specifically saved, up to the extent they are not repugnant of this Article, and are to continue until altered, repealed or modified or amended by the Parliament.[28]

THE PROTECTION OF CIVIL RIGHTS ACT

With an eye to eradicate pervasive discrimination practised against scheduled caste members, the Central Government of India enacted the Protectionof Civil Rights Act, 1955 (PCR Act) to enforce the abolition of "untouchability" under Article 17 of the constitution.[29] The PCR Act punishes offences that amount to the observance of "untouchability".[30] These include, inter alia, prohibiting entry into places of worship, denying access to shops and other public places, denying access to water supply, prohibiting entry into hospital, refusing to sell goods or water services, and insulting someone on the basis of his or her caste.[31]

PREVENTION OF ATROCITIES ACT, 1989

In 1989 the Scheduled Castes and Scheduled Tribes (Prevention of Atrocities) Act was enacted to prevent and punish caste- based abuses, to establish special courts for the trial of such offences and to provide for victim relief and rehabilitation.[32] The enactment of this act acknowledged the fact that abuses in their most violent and degrading form were still perpetrated against Dalit's decades after independence. The offences which are made punishable by this act depicts the retaliatory and customarily degrading treatment Dalits faced in daily lives. The offences include : forcing members of a scheduled caste to drink or eat any inedible or obnoxious substance; dumping excrement, waste matter, carcasses or any other obnoxious substance in their premises or neighbourhood; forcibly removing their cloths and parading them naked or with painted face or body; interfering with their rights to land; compelling a member of a scheduled caste into bonded labours; corrupting or fouling the water any spring, reservoir or any other source ordinarily used by scheduled castes; denying right of passage to a place of public resort; and using a position of dominance to exploit a scheduled caste woman sexually.[33]

HON'BLE COURTS JURISPRUDENCE ON UNTOUCHABILITY

Ambedkar said "If Untouchability is a sinful and immoral custom in the view of the Depressed classed it must be destroyed without any hesitation even if it was acceptable to the majority. This is the way in which all customs are dealt with by Courts of Law, if they find them to be immoral and against public policy."[34] The courts of India, have always followed the above dictum of Dr Ambedkar in order to deal with the cases related to untouchability.

In Surya Narayan Choudhary v State of Rajasthan[35], Rajasthan High Court strongly disapproved the prevailing practice of purification of Dalits alone before permitting them to enter into the temple for worship by making them wear 'Kanthimala', sprinkling 'gangajal' over them and giving them 'tulsidal'. The court ordered that the practice shall be discontinued as it violates the Article 14, 15, and 17 of the Constitution. C.J J.S. Verma in this case observed that "It is tragic that on the eve of Gandhi Jayanti we are debating a Harijans right to enter a public temple for worship as an equal; and directions of the Court be needed for enforcement of this right to equality. All men are born equal and the classification between them thereafter is manmade and artificial against the divine dictate. To present them as unequal before God is, therefore, injustice and an insult to our Maker besides being contrary to the guarantee and mandate of equality in our constitution and basic human right."

J. Subba Rao, in Basheshar Nath v Commissioner of Income Tax Delhi & Rajasthan[36], observed that "Article 17 illustrates the evil repercussion of the doctrine of waiver in its impact on the fundamental rights. That article in express terms forbids untouchability; obviously a person cannot ask the State to treat him as an untouchable."

Rajasthan High Court in Jay Singh v Union of India[37] discussed that Article 17 of the Constitution is similar to the 13th Amendment of the Constitution of the United States of America which abolished slavery. The Supreme Court in People's Union for Democrat Rights v Union of India[38] held that the fundamental right under Article 17 of the constitution is available against private individual and it is the duty of the state to ensure that this fundamental right does not get violated. In Bangalore W.C and Silk Mills v Mysore State, the high court held that imposition of 'untouchability" has no relation to the cause s which regulate certain classes of people beyond the pale of Caste estimate.[39]

CONCLUSION

Dr Ambedkar captured,the Dalit struggle as, "is a battle not for wealth or for power. It is a battle for freedom. It is a battle for the reclamation of human personality."[40]

Faced with abject poverty, oppression, exploitation and fear of the higher castes from whichthey earn their livings, Dalits have a very difficult time reporting atrocities, or otherviolations of law, and realizing their constitutional right to non-discrimination.The law as a mechanism for achieving social change has fallendrastically short of delivering on its paper promise of ensuring equality.[41]Among Dalits, the "Haves" are few and the "Have-Nots" aregreat. Regardless of class status, none have escaped the confiscation oftheir very persona or realized their right to self-determination in the mostprofound sense of the term: they remain stateless in their own countryand robbed daily of human dignity.The failure to address the inadequacies of the legal and reservation system implicate theGovernment of India's human rights obligations.India's remarkable affirmation of Dalit rights throughconstitutional privileges and legislative protections is a double-edgedsword. On the one hand, it lays the foundation for real socialtransformation. On the other hand, it masks the daily reality of de factosegregation, exploitation, and other forms of abuse by discouragingfurther scrutiny into the condition of Dalits.[42]Despite a large body of legislation andadministrative agency mandates assigned exclusively to deal with theoppression of scheduled castes, the laws have benefited few anddevelopment programs and welfare projects designed to improveeconomic conditions for Dalits have generally had little effect.Growing movements by Dalits to claim their basic humanrights and their human dignity are increasingly met with large-scaleviolence and attempts to further remove Dalits from economic self-sufficiency. However, it can be said in no uncertainty that The Constitution truly reflects the vison of welfare state with a view to ameliorating a historical injustice perpetrated on Scheduled Castes or Dalits.[43]While replying to the debate during the third (and final) reading of the Constitution on November 25, 1949, Dr Ambedkar made an eloquent and spell -binding speech in which he also reflected about the future. He said: "On the 26th of January 1950, we are going to enter into a life of contradictions. In politics we will have equality and in social and economic life we will have inequality. In politics we will be recognizing the principle of one man one vote and one vote one value. In our social and economic life, we shall, by reason of our social and economic structure, continue to deny the principle of one man one value. How long shall we continue to live this life of contradictions? How long shall we continue to deny equality in our social and economic life? If we continue to deny it for long, we will do so only by putting our political democracy in peril. We must remove this contradiction at the earliest possible moment or else those who suffer from inequality will blow up the structure of political democracy which this Assembly has so laboriously built up."[44]This is high time we pay a heed to these prophetic words in the interest of Indian democracy.

CHAPTER NINETEEN

ACCOUNTING OF REVENUE GENERATED FROM SALE OF NFTs: REGULATORY BLIND SPOT

Author: Kannu Upadhyaya, V year of B.A.,LL.B.(Hons.) from SVKM's NMIMS School of Law, Mumbai

We cannot start a discussion on Non Fungible Token (NFT) without talking through what it actually means. A NFT in simplest terms is a cryptographic asset backed with an unique identification number generated through blockchain network which allows the user to buy rare digital artifacts. As of now the concept is mostly applied to collectible arts. NFTs are becoming a popular platform for Indian artist to sell their art and generate revenue. Recently, from indie pop iconRitviz to legendary actor Amitabh Bachchanto captain of Indian Cricket team, Rohit Sharma made it to the news selling their NFTs for a whopping consideration as high as Seven Crore Indian Rupees[1]. Even the NFT backed cryptocurrency, like MANA, ENJ and similar sorts are all trading at an all-time high.The world's largest platform for selling NFTs, OpenSea, saw trade volume surge 950% in the last 30 days to hit $1.22 billion[2]. With everyone jumping in the sea of NFT it's hard not to question the accounting of revenue generate through sale of NFT for the purpose of taxation.

At present there are no accounting standards or statutory provisions specifically governing the accounting of revenue generate from saleof NFTs but it is pretty evident that revenue from sale of NFT would be a capital gain and hence would fall under income arising from capital receipts and not revenue receipts. The general principle of taxability of receipts under the Income Tax Act, 1960 (IT Act) is to tax income and not receipts[3] and hence as general principle capital receipts are not taxed unless specifically provided for under section 45 of the IT Act. Section 45 of the IT Act contemplates that "any profits or gains arising from the transfer of a capital asset affected in the previous year will be chargeable to income-tax under the head Capital Gains". First question that arrives in mind after reading the definition is what constitutes capital assets. In light of section 2(14) of the IT Act capital asset means"property of any kind held by an assesses, whether or not connected with his business or profession". The definition provided by the legislature is wide enough to encompasses almost all types of assets. For the purpose of taxation the Act further classifies assets into two sub categories of tangible and intangible assets. Revenue arising from intangible asset has always been a question of deliberation among the circle because, With the increasing complexitics of business structures and ever growing technology many new varieties of intangible assets keeps popping up and revenue from sale arising out of novel intangible digital assets, like NFT, consumer list and similar sorts end up escaping taxation altogether.It cannot also be denied,for all practical purposes that the Act cannot contemplate all types of capital receipts that would accrue; hence parliament keeps updating the Act to include new categories of intangible assets. Section 92(B) of the IT Act provides a list of intangible assets that in turn might help the assessors to determine what "transfer of capital asset" under section 45 of the IT Act would mean. However it is pertinent to note here that Section 92(B) of IT Act only provides an idea or helps in interpretation as this section applies to transfer pricing and not receipts particularly.

Since there is no statutory and judicial authority to regulate capital receipts arising out of sale of NFT. It brings us to an imperative issue, that whether in absence of any regulation how cana capital receipts transfer arising out of sale of NFT be valued or assessed for taxation. To better rephrases the last sentence and narrow down the scope even more, can the present jurisprudence of Section 45 of the IT Act assessa capital receipt arising out of sale of NFT. Section 45 of the IT Act mandates that two conditions must be satisfied in any transaction of a capital nature in order to lead to taxation under head of capital gain. Foremost, that the transaction must lcad to transfer of capital asset, either by sale or exchange or relinquishment of right or any asset or by compulsory acquisition under any law. Second, capital gains shall be determined in accordance with a formula as envisaged under Section 48 of the IT Acti.e. capital gains equals to sale consideration, less cost of acquisition less cost of improvements.

With respect to NFT being a self-generated asset it becomes nearly impossible to determine, cost of acquisition and without cost of acquisition no capital gain arises. The Hon'ble Supreme Court in case of PNB Finance ltd v/s. CIT[4] while citing a previous judgment of itself in CIT v/s B.C. Srinivas Shetty[5] held that all transactions as encompassed by section 45 of the IT Act on which capital computation of capital gains as provided under Section 48 of the IT Act i.e., capital gains equal to sale consideration, less cost of acquisition less cost of improvements, could not be applied, it must be regarded as "never intended as Section 45 to be a subject of charge".

Till now, the only limited power that the government can exercise to charge tax on capital receipt arising out of sale of NFT is through the assessor as he can invoke the "substance over form" test. The underlying assumption in applying substance over form test is that the transaction engaged by a person or business entity should not hide its true intent[6]. When it comes to NFT the intent can be excessively hard to determine as none of the companies and/or individuals are engaged in the business of selling or buying collectibles NFTs.In addition, the Government very recently introduced General Anti Avoidance Regulation (GAAR), to deal with particularly those transaction which are entered into by entities, with sole purpose of tax avoidance. GAAR could be very difficult to implement in case of NFT as it applies only on transactions with a commercial purpose. In case of Buying and selling of NFT it becomes nearly impossible to ascertain a commercial purpose as it's a one off transaction having a bonafide purpose. The Government of India has recently proposed to bring forward The Cryptocurrency and Regulation of Official Digital Currency Bill, 2021 which inter alia seeks to prohibit all private cryptocurrencies in India. The bill can be a powerful tool to bring forth the regulation or some sort of clarity in buying and selling of collectibles NFT. Alternatively in the upcoming budget of 2022,IT Act can be also be amended to bring in NFTs or cryptocurrency backed assets as intangible assets. Currently there exists no clarity on taxation of income from sale of NFTs and Government is also losing on huge tax revenue. It would be interesting to observe what steps the Government takes to regulate revenue generation.

CHAPTER TWENTY

VIOLENCE AGAINST WOMEN

Author: Monu Yadav, pursuing B.B.A.,LL.B. from Geeta Institute of Law,

Monu Yadav

Violence against women and girls is defined as any act of gender based violence that results physical, sexual or mental harm or suffering to women and girls. Violence against women and girls takes many different forms, including domestic violence – sexual assault and harassment, child marriage, sex trafficking so called 'horror' crimes and female genital mutilation. It is rooted in the gender inequality that women face throughout their lives from childhood to her old age. It is the most widespread violation of human rights that effects badly to the women life and their communities.

Rapes and non-consensual sexual activities from a large portion of the violence committed against women. Rape is typically the sexual intercourse carried on the women without her consent. Marital rape is also the example of violence against women. It is a non-consensual sexual intercourse carried on between the married couples. Husbands often impose and force themselves upon their wives without her consent. It leads to great deal of abuse and physical molestation committed upon women body. Women have fear of violence in their mind which causes lack of women participation. Fear of violence in the mind of women has been so deep which cannot be out easily. Women have always been considered as a thing of enjoyment in our society. They are the victims of humiliation, exploitation and torture. From the origin of social life in the world so manycenturies came and gone but people's mind and their environment a lot, but violence against women is not seems to change a bit. According to National Crimes Records Bureau, single woman is raped every 20 minutes.

A big incident of violence happened in Delhi on 16th of December in 2012, a lady of 23 years old got raped by brutal gang. A huge crowd of anger people come out of street and they call for change. The census of 2012 shoes that the crime against women is near about 64% which means average within three minutes a women face violence. In rural areas, the bride usually belonging to a poor household is unable to meet the groom's high demand for the dowry money. They fail to pay the amount groom ask for. In such cases women also faces verbal and physical abuse of groom. The women is beaten and abused for her family's incapability to fulfil the dowry. The cases of dowry death are mostly seen in rural areas,even after happening such type of cases regularly in the society, it is not going to change the societal norms against women. These cases happened even after increasing educational level of the people. Such cases happen because of inefficient legal system and weak rules of law. According to research it was found that violence against women begins at her homes in the rural areas by the family members, relatives, neighbours and friends.At least 155 countries have passed laws on domestic violence and 140 have legislation on sexual harassment in their work place. But challenges remain enforcing this laws, the amount of violence committed against women are still increasing day by day.

- 35% of women suffered violence through her husband and from their families.
- Approximately 650 million women alive in the today world got married at the age of 15.
- Globally 38% of murders of women are committed by an intimate partner.
- And near about 200 million women have experience female genital mutilation.

Violence against women is a blot on the nation and the society also. As long as the women are subjected to violence, the international image of the country is also going to suffer. Also, incident of domestic violence, sexual assaults and other crimes on the women will continuously damages country and obstructs national progress. Therefore, it is the imperative to take stringent counter measures to diminish any kind of violence against women.Ending violence against women is critical to achieving sustainable development. Decades of progress and millions of lives are at stake. Keeping gender based violence at the top of the government agendas and engaging the public is more important than ever. Advocate for more youth violence prevention programs. Get others to speak out against sexual violence stop your sexual advances if the other person says no and encourage others to do the same. The spotlight Initiative a global partnership between European Union and the United Nation, has worked to eliminate all forms of violence against women. It is committed to shift people mind by –

- Drawing attention on gender discrimination.
- Working to change the social norms and practices.
- Increasing public awareness.
- Creating space for activities and survivors to share their stories.
- Educating communities about sexual and gender based violence.

CHAPTER TWENTY-ONE

CONSUMER PROTECTION ACT, 2019- CRITICAL ANALYSIS

Author: U. Sai Sahithi Sri, II year of B.A.,LL.B. from Symbiosis Law School, Hyderabad

Introduction

A consumer is the one who buys goods and services, therefore consumer protection is nothing but protecting rights of consumers against malpractices practiced in the market. The term consumerism emerged in the 1960s and was denoted as a set of social forces which aimed to create pressures on business entities in order to ensure marketplace practices are in the interest of consumers. In order to maintain this kind of pressure on business entities so that consumer's interest can be upheld, consumer protection laws were formed in the interest of consumers. One of the main reasons behind framing such laws is to curb the increasing unfair market malpractices. Some of these unfair practices are- misbranding, adulteration, spurious products, fictitious pricing, deceptive packaging, black marketing, false and misleading advertisements etc.....

Well the other reason behind bringing such laws is to empower the consumers and to safeguard consumer's life from the hazards of spurious goods and adulteration etc... These laws also make sure that the consumer gets to know about the information which is required regarding that particular service or product so that he can decide whether he can choose it or not. These are the reasons behind bringing consumer laws and policies. When it comes to the case of India the evolution of consumer protection laws can be divided into 3 parts. Pre- 1950, 1950-1986 and 1986- present. Before 1950, the issues regarding consumer protection was managed through the provisions present in the English Common Law. The English Common Law provided three categories under which different aspects of consumer protection were dealt, but these categories were not named explicitly. Those three categories which were granted by the British legal structure were a) Torts, b) Contracts and c) Fiduciary Obligations.

Later on, after 1950, when the constitution came into force, the central government enacted several laws to deal with different problems of consumer protection. These provisions were limited to the subject matter of each statute. The consumer had to establish relevance with at least one of these laws and if suppose he was unable to establish such thing then he had to file the matter under torts or contracts or under fiduciary obligations. There were totally ten kinds of different acts which were enacted to take care of different aspects of consumer protection but none of them were unable to properly achieve the objective of safeguarding consumer rights. Later on, based on the frame work laid down by the United Nations, CPA, 1986 was enacted by the parliament. This act created separate platforms for the redressal by mandating a series of courts to deal with problems faced by the consumers. Further the act was amended three times in the years 1991, 1993 and 2002. These amendments enhanced the scope of authority given to the consumer courts.

Since then nearly after 3 decades the act got replaced by Consumer Protection Act, 2019. The aim of this new act is to deal with consumer problems in an efficient and quick manner. The idea of the legislature behind enacting new act instead of amending the old act was to grant a high degree of security to the interests of consumer. The need of this new act arises from the very fact that due to rapid growth of digital technology, e- commerce etc... the nature of business modes has changed which have adversely affected the interests of consumers. Adding to this, the frame work of consumer protection act, 1986 and guidelines set by consumer affairs ministry were not adequate to deal with such issues, hence new act addressing these issues is enacted. Hence, the old act got replaced by the new act based on the need of current society. These days most of the population in our country is doing online shopping at a large scale; it means that there is a dire need of laws which protect consumers who does online shopping.

According to a particular statics it was projected that nearly 329 million Indian citizens are buying online which means that nearly 70% of the population shop online. Recently during the pandemic according to a study it was shown that 86% Indians have adopted online shopping which indicates accelerated adoption of E-Commerce in the country. So by this it can be deciphered that there is a need of consumer laws which also mentions about E- commerce as well. Hence, Consumer Protection Act, 2019 has been introduced with inclusion of new aspects and modified characteristics to protect the rights of consumer in current Indian Scenario. The researcher tries to study about the Consumer Protection Act, 2019 in detail and tries to find out its advantages and disadvantages.

Main Features of Consumer Protection Act, 2019

Consumer Protection Act, 2019 is a replacement of Consumer Protection Act, 1986. Let us know what are the aspects which are replaced by this amendment act?

The following aspects are introduced through the act-

Change in the term Consumer- Through 2019 act, the definition of consumer has been widened. These days online shopping is randomly increasing in India. So, in this case to protect the people who shop online, online customers are also included in the definition of Consumer. Through this e-commerce market is included in the act and consumer protection laws are made applicable to it. This definition considers a person as consumer if he/she avails a service or buys any goods for their self use. All kinds of online/offline transactions done through teleshopping or direct selling or multi-level marketing or through electronic means are mentioned as ways through which a consumer can buy or hire any goods, services etc...

Change in the definition of goods- According to CPA, 1986, definition of goods does not include food. Now through the CPA 2019 act, food is also included under the definition of goods. Now all the food selling platforms are included under the ambit of CPA, 2019. This step is a progressive one because these day's people are buying lots of food from outside due to busy life schedule; in this case through this act their rights are protected to ensure that they have a good food.

Change in the term services- These day's people are turned towards telecom services hence telecom has been added under the definition of services through 2019 act. It would be still better if they would have added as telecommunication services instead of telecom as per TRA, act.

Pecuniary Jurisdiction of Consumer courts- Now the limit of the amount in a case has been increased to be dealt by the consumer courts. Now a district forum can deal with a case which involves a sum of Rs.20 lakh to Rs.1cr. In the same way a state commission can deal with the cases which includes an amount of Rs.1cr to Rs. 10cr. Now, the cases which are dealt by National commission involve a sum which is above Rs.10cr.

Unfair trades/ Contracts- If there is a contract between a supplier/ manufacturer/ serviced provider and consumer which might cause harm to the consumer then such contracts can be called as unfair contracts. For ex- If one of the parties terminates the contract without even informing the other party due to which the party suffers loss then such contracts are called as unfair contracts.

Product Liability- Through this act now a person can even sue for the emotional pain which he suffered through the product service which he brought. Now the person can file a suit against both manufacturer and seller for the emotional distress which he/she suffered due to the product.

Misleading Advertisements- If there is a false representation of the products through advertisements then in that case endorser who advertised that product and manufacturer of that product will be punished under this CPA, 2019. Before endorsing the product endorser needs to verify all the claims of the product, in case if the endorser is proved guilty in CCPA investigation then he/she may be fined with Rs10 lakhs which may increase up to Rs.50 lakhs. The act also stated that the endorser and manufacturer may also be punished with an imprisonment of 2years.

Mediation- This new act introduces mediation cell branches in each state which helps in resolving the disputes easily. This branch helps to reduce the burden on consumer courts which have to deal with many cases. This kind of mode helps in resolving the disputes quickly.

Central Consumer Protection Authority (CCPA) – Through CPA,2019, CCPA has been established to deal with protection of consumer rights. CCPA is the authority which deals with the protection of consumer rights. This authority is responsible for introducing new plans and process through which consumers can be protected from the harms arising from the products/ from unfair trade practices etc... The main objective behind setting this authority is to render suggestions regarding promotion and protection of consumer rights under CPA, 2019.

At the same time CCPA possess powers through which they can recall products or withdrawal from services which are dangerous in nature. Through the means of CPA, 2019 each state shall have a State Consumer Protection Council also known as State Council. At the same time each district will consist of District Council which shall be governed by that respective District Collector.

Provisions regarding appeals

Only if the case involves substantial law of question, then such cases can be appealed from state commission to national commission. On the other hand appeals can be made from National Commission to Supreme Court only if the case is originated in National Commission.

Jurisdiction- Consumer can file cases in the place where he/she resides or works. Now consumer commission jurisdictions are expanded in order to accept the complaints made by the complainant where he/she resides or works. This has been introduced through the Consumer Protection Act, 2019.

Inclusion of E-Commerce Platforms

According to Consumer Protection Act, 2019, e-commerce shall be governed by all those laws which are applicable in case of direct selling of a service or product. Now all the e-commerce sites are supposed to disclose the details of seller's number, email Id, website etc... There are also penalties if counterfeit products are sold on these platforms.

The New act also mention s few rights of the consumers, they are-

- Right to be protected against the marketing of goods or services which can be hazardous to life and property
- Right to be informed about the quality, quantity, potency, purity, standard and price of goods, products and services
- Right to be assured of access to goods, products and services at competitive prices.
- Right to be heard at appropriate forums
- Right to seek redressel against unfair trade practices that are involved in exploitation of customers
- Right to consumer awareness[i]

Challenges Present in Consumer Protection Act, 2019

Central Consumer Protection Authority- In case of CCPA the authority to investigate and head the investigative wing is vested upon Director General. Now this authority is given to District Collectors who are supposed to govern these issues. This makes the functions of this authority as vague because collector is given with all these responsibilities. Now he/she is supposed to take care of this investigative wing and as well as job of collector which might overlap and in turn it would result into the clash of his/her interests.

Ambiguity in case of Appealing- CCPA has authority to penalize endorsers, manufactures for misleading advertisements etc... But to appeal against such orders, it can only be done in national commission. But for the basis for hearing such appeals is uncertain which leaves the consumers and legal fraternity in a great confusion. It is also ambiguous whether the disputes with the present consumer commission will be heard by the same or will it be transferred to the courts having pecuniary jurisdictions as per the new act. This kind of loophole may lead to further delay of the cases.

Mediation- In the case of mediation, time period is not mentioned within which a case must be resolved. This may lead to delay in the disposal of a case.

Services- Under the definition of services the new act fails to include medical and educational services. Since, the 1986 acts there were several conflicting judgments regarding medical services, but the act did not include these services. This act could include those educational services which can be treated as consumer service, but it failed to mention them. On the other hand the definition services include "Telecom Services' which may prove as a drawback. This is because according to the Telecom Regulatory Authority of India Act, 1997[ii] uses the term telecommunication service and provides a wider definition which consists of all the matters related to it. When it comes to the CPA, 2019, it is mentioned as only 'Telecom Service' which has a narrow coverage and also may exclude internet, cellular and other related services.

Exclusion of Health Care Services- In the case of Indian Medical Association v V.P. Shantha[iii] and others, the apex court stated that services rendered by medical practitioners come under the purview of service under CPA, 1986. But if suppose the service was of free of charge then it shall not be considered under the Act. Now it can be said that even apex court has recognized these services under the act, but still 2019 act fails to expressly mention the same under the definition of services. It is said that at first, when health care services was included in consumer protection bill, 2018, medical professionals and communities opposed that stating this can be misused against them if these services are placed under the ambit of the act.

Hence, the term 'health care services" was deleted from the definition of services. When this is being questioned, the govt. officials are stating that though the term is not mentioned still consumers can go to consumer forums and file complaint in the case of medical negligence or deficiency in medical services. According to the phrase "includes, but not limited to" mentioned under sec 2(42) of CPA, 2019, it can be said that this is an inclusive section and still medical services can be added to it.

If govt. authority leaves this section without including medical services and on the other hand if it mentions that consumers can still file complaints in case of deficiency in medical services, then such things might collide with each other during the interpretation of the clause.

Exclusion of Educational Services- According to CPA, 2019, these services are not mentioned under the ambit of service definition. When it was claimed that why can't they can be mentioned under the ambit of CPA, 1986. It was referred to a judgment delivered by the Hon'ble Supreme Court in the case of Maharshi Dayanand University v. Surjeet Kaur[iv], in which it stated that educational institutions cannot be treated as commodities, and mentioned that these institutions are not providing any kind of services, hence there can be no question of deficiency of service. Hence they cannot fall under the purview of CPA, 1986. But on the other hand National and State consumer forums gave several judgments in the favor of students recognizing them as consumers.

In the case of Jai Kumar Mittal vs. Briliant Tutorials,[v] it was held that defective study material sent by institution falls under the ambit of deficiency of service. In the case of Sonal Matapurkar v. S. Niglingappa Institute,[vi] a dental institute had taken admissions more than sanctioned seats due to which students were not allowed to take examinations. In this case, National Commission held that even though the students had paid the money they were not allowed to take exam which indicates that there was a deficiency in the service of Institution. Hence the institution was ordered to return back donations to the students.

From the above case laws it can be deciphered that educational services can be included under the ambit of CPA, 2019. This is because students are beneficiaries in case of availing these services but at the same time all kind of educational services cannot be included under the act. If it is a case of giving defective study materials, negligence in allotting roll numbers, hall tickets and other activities etc... it may fall under the ambit of deficiency in service. But when a complaint is filed upon unreasonable grounds then such cases can be excluded from the act. Hence a clear demarcation must be placed in between educational activities which may fall under CPA, 2019 and which may not. This may help to protect consumer rights and increases efficiency in educational services.

District consumer commissions are established for the sake of convenience of consumers who want to file a case, but the same thing is lacking in the case of filing suits in case of unfair trades. This is because any complaints regarding unfair trades or contracts can only be filed in state or national commissions. This might impose hurdles on the consumers who are comfortable in approaching District Commission.

Conclusion and Suggestions

Conclusion

Consumer Protection Act, 2019 is really appreciable because it includes several aspects which are required in present situation. This act has made several progressive steps by introducing CCPA, widening the ambit of pecuniary jurisdictions, mediation and increasing the scope of services etc... All these things are required in order to protect consumer rights in today's digital world. Though this act has come up with several progressive steps, it also failed to mention few aspects which cannot be made unseen. For example this act has not provided with the duties and power possessed by the Director-General of CCPA. The kind of power he/she shall possess is still unclear. The act also doesn't mention medical & educational services under the definition of the term "services". Hence, inclusion of such services might end the ambiguity and conflicts arising from the interpretation of the provision. To make this act successful it must be properly implemented.

Suggestions

Following are few suggestions which can be implemented-

1) Services like medical and education must be included under the definition of Services under the Consumer Protection Act, 2019.

2) Instead of mentioning as "telecom services" under the ambit of services in the CPA, 2019, they can be mentioned as telecommunication services which may widen its ambit and mentions all other related services.

3) A proper period of time must be stipulated in case of mediation which ensures that cases get resolved within a particular period of time. This may reduce the delay in deciding cases.

4) Govt. should not favor few professionals as it was done in the case of deleting medical services from the CPA, 2019. Govt. should give utmost importance to the consumer's rights.

5) People should be made aware of this act by conducting awareness programs and campaigns, in order to make people realize their rights and to have a successful implementation of this act.

6) A clear demarcation should be laid down upon the types of educational services which can be included under CPA, 2019 through which consumer rights can be availed by the students.

CHAPTER TWENTY-TWO

HATE SPEECH

Author: Rishant Solanki, I year of B.B.A.,LL.B. from The NorthCap University

Any form of expression through which the speaker has intention to defame, humiliate, or show hatred against a particular person or a group based on religion, skin color, gender identity, or nationality is called Hate speech.

IS HATE SPEECH FREE SPEECH IN INDIA?

Latestly, Yati Narsighnanad (Deepak Tyagi), a Hindu priest got arrested by Uttarakhand police on January 15, in two separate cases which include Haridwar hate speech in which his speech roar for annihilation against Muslims, and the second one is for his defaming remarks against women.

The people in our society believes in stereotypes and these stereotypes made people to believe that another individual who belongs to different cast, class, religion, sex is inferior to them and do not enjoy the same amount of respect and dignity as them the obstinate to adhere to a particular believe without carrying for the sentiments rights faith of others to co-exist peacefully make the hate speech more derogatory.

PROVISIONS OF HATE SPEECH IN INDIA

The constitution of our country has provided us freedom of speech and expression under article 19(1)(a) as a fundamental right but this right is not absolute some limitations are inflicted by article 19(2) this is also understandable that claim to free speech ends where hate speech begins.

Under Indian penal code section such as 153A ,153B ,295A,505(1), and 505(2) are concerned with hate speech. Under the Representation of People act 1951 (RPA) section 8 states: prevents a person convicted of the illegal use of the freedom of speech from contesting an election. Section 123(3A) and 125 are also about hate speech in reference to elections and electoral practices.

COMMITTEE SUGGESTIONS FOR CHANGES IN IPC

According to Bezbaruah Committee 2014,an amendment to section 153 C and 509 A of IPC which is punishable by five years and fine or both and punishable by three years or fine or both respectively. Another committee instituted in 2019 under T.K. Viswanathan had recommended inserting section 153 C(b) and section 505 A in the IPC for urging to commit an offence on the grounds of caste, race, gender, place of birth, language, religion, community. It proposed punishment of up to two years along with rupees 5,000 fine.

GRAVE CONSEQUENCES OF HATE SPEECH

Hate speech can harm individual communities and societies. The targets of hate speech often experience negative emotional, physical, and mental upshot. This can include low self-worth, anxiety, fear for their lives, harms to dignity, and suicide. Hate speech has resulted in cyber bulling which often attacks minority population based on religion.Several instances of online disinformation are leading centered around social struggles around race and ethnicity, deepening these social rifts through use of hate speech. It causes mob lynching and honor killing. Presence of these kind of activities in a country is a serious challenge to its Democratic character. It can damage the image of a country at the International forum.

ROLE PLAYED BY THE SUPREME COURT

The apex court of our country has given pivotal judgements in various fields also in hate speech areas, in the latest judgmentsupreme court held that, historical truth just be depicted without in any way encouraging Hatred between different communities. In Shery Singhal v. union of India: Concerns were raised about section 66A of the information act ,2000 relating to the fundamental right of free and expression where the court differentiate between discussion advocacy, insighting and held that first two were essence of article 19(1).

S. Rangarajan Etc.V/S P. Jagjivan Ram: In this case the supreme court verdict that freedom of expression cannot be censored unless the situation so created is menacing to the public interest.

The existence of hate speech is not a new fact by any stretch of imagination butwith theoccurrence of multiple platforms,for instance social media, where anyone can deliver hate speech without any fear and hesitation.Good amount of hate has been perpetuated through platform like Facebook, twitter, YouTube, Instagram. One of the prominent instances is persecution of Rohingya Muslims by Myanmar military junta. The calls for violence against Rohingya on Facebookand the brass-necked killings in Myanmar have led bare the connection between two as investigated by multiple journalists.

<u>WAY FORWARD</u>

Hate speech is often delivered against marginalist classes and the people who are already a minority section due to there race, language, religion. The most effective way to dilute hatred is by the means of education it has a prominent role in promoting, understandingand sympathizing with others. Fight against hate speech cannot be done in isolation it needs wider platform such as United nation where it should be discussed, and the necessary steps should be taken. All the responsible government, regional bodies and other agencies should take hate speech as a matter of concern and threat to the unity and integrity of a country. Alternative mechanisms or department should be established to tackle and prevent the fire of hate speech.

CHAPTER TWENTY-THREE

ANALYSING THE INDIAN GAMING LAW AND POLICY IN LIGHT OF THE RECENT TIMES

Author: Sabaat Fatima, III year of B.A.,LL.B. from School of Law, HILSR, Jamia Hamdard

Introduction

Playing games is enjoyed by all age groups of people across the world for entertainment purposes. Presently, the Indian gaming industry is the most exciting industry making increased investments from consumers and companies. Since time immemorial gambling has been a part of Indian culture. The mention of gambling can be traced to the times of Mahabharata where the rivals were tested by their skill at the board and dice games rather than through wars. Since the evolution of television and online gaming modes, the gaming industry has witnessed an exemplary shift. The Modi Government sponsored the Digital India Drive[i] has improved the infrastructure by and large. The enhancement in the internet speed in the remote and rural areas had led to the consumption of more content. If we talk about the festivals then there is a religious connotation that gambling during Diwali is auspicious, even the Courts in India[ii] held that gambling is not an offence if it takes place among friends and not in the gambling house or a public place. Hence, gambling is not considered an offence in Diwali. Since the 1970s, Indian gaming has been a centre of political controversies, as the debate usually revolved around the morality or immorality of gambling. A study conducted by KPMG[iii] India stated that the future of the Indian online gaming industry will be redefined by the digitization of traditional Indian games by 2024. On the other hand, the game developers have created the content of games in different local and traditional languages, examples of such games are Rummy, Teen Patti and Poker.

The concept of gaming in India and the need for the law

The Indian population is extremely passionate about sports and sports-related exercises. Indian games have a lift as internet gaming has changed physical games into virtual games, e-games, e-sports, online games, fantasy sports, and so forth. As of date, we have no devoted online gaming and online gambling laws in India. Additionally, we have not committed fantasy sports law in India till now and as such, they are included under the current game laws and as such online poker, online rummy, online lotteries are as yet not governed by any devoted Indian law. The outcome is inescapable, for example, online games in India are in an in-between state and legitimate inconveniences.

Gambling in India is limited aside from particular classes including lotteries and pony horse racing. Opponents of gambling claim that it prompts crime, corruption, and money laundering, while proponents of gambling contend that it tends to be a huge source of income for the state. For instance, casinos in Goa[iv] generated Rs 135 Crore to the state revenue in 2013. The Public Gambling Act[v] of 1867 is a central law that restricts running or being accountable for a public gambling house. The punishment which will be imposed on violating this law will be a fine of Rs 200 or imprisonment of as long as 3 months.

Except for Orissa and Assam, all other states have excluded games of skill from gambling laws. Online gambling in India is still a debatable discussion and there is no determination on the issue of online gambling yet. In 2019[vi], a boy in Hyderabad hanged himself to death and the reason for his death was that his mother used to scold him to stop playing a very known game PUBG.

Another incident took place in Hyderabad where a 16-year-old boy hanged himself to death from a ceiling fan[vii]. It was reported that his father used to scold him for wasting time on games rather than studying for his English exam. His father demanded a ban on the game PUBG.

The Press Trust of India News Agency[viii] reported that two men in their twenties were playing a game on their phones near a railway track in Maharashtra and were killed by an oncoming train. There was a massive storm in India after these incidents and the people demanded to ban the game as it was causing distraction, violence and hatred. In Gujarat[ix], some cities banned the game but the youngsters were still violating the ban. A petition[x] was filed by the Internet freedom foundation in the Gujarat High Court to declare the ban unconstitutional. It was also claimed that to ban the game is an extreme step as there must be some other way to handle the situation because you cannot call someone criminal just because they are playing a video game. Hence, the ban was lifted.

Another very popular game was Pokémon Go[xi] which now needs no introduction. The internet was flooded with cases about its interactivity and stories of mishaps and freak incidents. The Pokémon Go security strategy permits Niantic to share collected data and non-distinguishing data with outsiders for research and investigation, segment profiling and other comparative purposes. How Niantic itself can utilize this data is likewise left not entirely clear. But the fact that players have to hold their phones in front of them to play causes them to be distracted from their surroundings and has prompted mishaps. Also, different Pokémon characters and Pokéstops (destination of in-game items) were situated on private property, which expected users to enter private property to get them. Under Indian law, what Pokémon Go players did would not be viewed as criminal trespass, because there was no intention to harm. Notwithstanding, the tort of trespass to land will be applied as soon as there is an unjustifiable entry into another's private property. A study[xii] found that if more than 750 users play this game, 85% of them admitted to playing while driving a car, and more than 10% admitted to intruding while playing. To additionally entangle matters, the game was not released officially in India. The issue raised was if it has not been officially released then how the people were playing?

The dare-based "game", Blue Whale Challenge[xiii], spread over 50 days, the challenge allegedly orders participants to complete 50 tasks that include self-hurt, body mutilation and watching startling videos. As the game lifts, participants reach the final day that probably ends up in suicide. The contestants must prove that they have finished the tasks by sending proof — pictures and videos to their "director" or the "whale" who had been instructing them all this while. The challenge has reportedly claimed over 130 deaths so far, with multiple youngsters suicides in India[xiv]. Unauthorized versions of the apps were being downloaded by the users. Other than their provisions on IP, the applicable terms of service require users to sign away various rights. The provision that has the most consideration is an obligatory arbitration clause, which expects clients to forgo their right to sue except if they quit by email or standard mail within 30 days of downloading the application. This is a critical issue in jurisdictions.

In 2013, the game was started in Russia and reported to cause the first suicide in 2015. A former psychology student, Philipp Budeikin was expelled from the university because he invented this game. According to him, he aimed to clean society by pushing those people to suicide who considered themselves valueless. He was detained and sentenced to three years of imprisonment for abetting at least 16 teenagers to kill themselves.

The first case in India was reported when a 14-year old boy jumped from the seventh floor of a building and hence died. Another case was reported in West Bengal, where a class X student committed suicide. His body was found in the washroom with his face covered with a plastic bag. The Ministry of Electronics and IT directed internet platforms like Facebook, Google, Instagram, Yahoo and WhatsApp to remove the links to the online game. The Ministry of Women and Child Development filed a petition demanding a ban on the online game.

An overview of the existing legal framework regulating the gambling industry in India

Laws that are affecting the content in games

Following is a list of laws that control the contents[xv] and graphics that can be added to a game.

Pornographic and obscenity laws

Indian games and gaming websites include contents that may be regarded objectionable under the pornographic and obscenity laws of India. Some websites offer games that have animated caricatures of human beings especially outraging the modesty of women in such a way that may be construed as offensive as per the moral standards of India.

i. Indian Penal Code, 1860 and the Information Technology Act, 2008

The Indian Penal Code[xvi] ("IPC") and the Information Technology Act, 2008[xvii] ("IT Act") punish the publication and transmission of obscene content. The IPC inter alia restricts the deal, show and circulation of obscene content and punishes any individual who associates with the advertisement, offers, or attempts to do any vulgar action. The IT Act inter alia punishes the transmission of any vulgar content or explicitly express content in electronic structure, including child pornography content.

ii. Indecent Representation of Women

The Indecent Representation of Women (Prohibition) Act[xviii], 1986 restricts any obscene representation of women for example featuring the figure of a lady, her structure or body that aim to disrespect the class or pride of women, or that are responsible to ruin or harm the public morality or ethics. The punishment for infringing the provisions of the Indecent Representation of Women (Prohibition) Act, 1986 is imprisonment for a term of up to two years and a fine of up to INR 2,000.

Laws Affecting Action-based and Violent Games

Famous games like Call of Duty, Grand Theft Auto etc, display action-based games[xix] which are appealing to youngsters. The linkage between the exposure of such games to teens and the violence happening in society has still not been taken into notice by the Indian Courts. Though states like the USA, Europe and other Asian countries have earlier passed regulations to control the sale of specific video games to children the Supreme Court of the US quashed it by saying that video games possess the constitutional right to free speech and hence cannot be controlled. 'PlayerUnknown's Battlegrounds', or 'PUBG' is a new contestant in the multiplayer social gaming space that has created an uproar and also doubts on how suitable it is for children to play. AhadNizam, an 11-year old boy from Mumbai filed a PIL before the Bombay High Court claiming that PUBG promotes violence, murder, aggression, looting, gaming addiction and cyberbullying and hence it should be banned.

Intellectual Property Right Issues

Games are frequently theme-based in nature and use pictures, musical notes, figures, characters etc. to add to the allure of the games. All these works are liable to copyright protection in their own right; using such copyrighted material in the games, without taking permissions/licenses from the owner of copyrighted material, can activate copyright infringement issues under the Copyright Act, 1957[xx]. The copyright owner can take civil or criminal action. Famous titles should be protected under the Trade Mark Act, 1999[xxi].

Personality Rights Issues

To allure, the gamers for some games such as the FIFA series or the Fallout Franchise, utilize the caricatures, likeness, voice, reputation or popularity of a celebrity for benefitting their business without any approval from the celebrity. This may lead to infringing the personality rights[xxii] of the celebrity. Personality rights have still not been perceived by the

Indian Courts. In the case of ShivajiRaoGaikwad v Varsha Productions[xxiii], the praised actor 'Rajinikanth' sought an interim injunction stopping the Defendant from utilizing his name, image, style or caricature in the film "Main HoonRajinikanth" and other impending movies to violate his copyright or invade his personality rights. The Madras High Court ordered an interim injunction and put a stay on the release of the film. However, the name of the film was later changed to "Main HoonRajini". Similarly, games utilizing celebrity images, caricatures, voices, etc. without any permission, may be held to be violating the particular celebrity's personality rights.

Social gaming and telecom laws

SMS Marketing Related Laws- Considering different complaints made against spam calls and SMSes, the Telecom Regulatory Authority of India ("TRAI")[xxiv] issued the Telecom Commercial Communications Customer Preference Regulations, 2010[xxv] which looks to forbid the Unsolicited Commercial Communications ("UCC"). Telecom Commercial Communications Customer Preference Regulations, 2018[xxvi] replaced the 2010 Regulations. The TCCCPR has the following broad requirements to be followed with commercials communication:-

Opt-out/Consent- The TCCCPR accommodates an opt-out process for business correspondence, where clients may enlist their inclinations in regards to inter alia, the accompanying (I) the sort of messages/calls will get (eg. SMS, Voice Call, Robo Call, and so on) (ii) the time when they will get business communications; (iii) which day of the week they will get the business communications.

Transactional communications- Transactional messages/calls might be sent whether or not the client is in the somewhat or completely blocked category. A transactional message, for example, a message set off by a transaction by a client who is a client of the sender ought not to fall inside the ambit of unsolicited commercial communication and an induced assent from the client should do the trick. Transactional communications ought to be sent to the client within 30 minutes of the transaction being performed and ought to be straightforwardly identified with the transaction.

Header/Content Template- Senders might have the option to send business communications just through an enrolled 'header' allotted to it for the said reason by the Access Provider. A header is an alphanumeric linc of the most extreme eleven characters or numbers allocated to an individual, business or lawful entity to send business communications. The

TCCCPR takes into account the name or number to be utilized instead of a header. Such headers may likewise vary for transactional and promotional communications sent even by a similar client.

Activation of Value Added Services- After different grumblings in regards to the activation of value-added services ("VAS") without the approval of supporters and the subsequent allowance in the equilibrium of the endorsers, the TRAI ordered explicit guidelines to guarantee that purchasers are not charged erroneously/excessively for any VAS. The TRAI has forced different obligations on telecom administrators including:

- Educating the consumer through SMS, on the enactment of a VAS, the legitimacy time of such help, the charges for reestablishment and the strategy for the buyer to withdraw from the assistance;
- Before subscribing to a VAS, the administrator should acquire affirmation from the purchaser through an SMS within 24 hours of activation of the VAS. The customer should be charged just if such affirmation is received failing which, the VAS should be ceased;
- If a VAS is offered through WAP or mobile internet, unequivocal assent of the purchaser is required through an online ascent entryway as detailed in TRAI's ways.

Although the TRAI has put all these duties on telecom administrators we have seen that most VAS agreements between the game developers and telecom administrators commonly include the telecom administrator giving its duties to the VAS supplier. Further, telecom administrators commonly likewise require the VAS supplier to conform to every single appropriate law and further repay the telecom administrator in case of any misfortune/punishment.

<u>Other laws that affect the gaming industry</u>

Foreign Direct Investment & Foreign Technology Collaborations in Gambling Industry

The Foreign Direct Investment Policy ("FDI Policy") of India released by the Ministry of Commerce & Industry, Government of India, Foreign Direct Investment ("FDI") is restricted[xxvii] in elements associated in;

- lottery, private lottery, online lotteries, etc; and
- Gambling and betting including casinos, etc.

The expressions "lottery, gambling and betting" have not been defined under the FDI Policy[xxviii]. For breaching the FDI Policy, one may have to pay a punishment of up to threefold the entirety included where such sum is quantifiable, or up to INR 2, 00,000 where the sum isn't quantifiable, and where the negation is a proceeding with one, further punishment which may reach out to INR 5,000 for consistently after the primary day during which the repudiation proceeds. As of late, there has been a gigantic flood in foreign direct investment in elements offering games prevalent on the skill, including Rummy and fantasy sports.

Restrictions under Exchange Control Regulations

Under the Foreign Exchange Management Act, 1999[xxix] ("FEMA") read with Foreign Exchange Management (Current Account Transaction) Rules, 2000[xxx] ("Current Account Rules"), settlement of pay from rewards from a lottery, dashing/riding or some other side interest is restricted.

Intermediary Guidelines Notified under the IT Act

The Information Technology (Intermediaries guidelines) Rules, 2011 ("Intermediary Guidelines")[xxxi] were notified under the IT Act in April 2011. This requires delegates like ISPs and different mediators to inter alia notice vital due tirelessness and distribute rules and guidelines and user agreements for access or use of the transfer speed given by the intermediary. The term 'intermediary' has been characterized under the IT Act to incorporate "telecom specialists, network specialist organizations, web access suppliers, web-facilitating specialist co-ops, web crawlers, online installment locales, online-closeout destinations, online-commercial centres and cyber cafes".In the milestone judgment of Shreya Singhal v. Union of India[xxxii] ("ShreyaSinghal"), known for the Supreme Court striking down the disputable Section 66A[xxxiii] of the IT Act, the Supreme Court additionally read down the arrangements of the Intermediary Guidelines identified with blocking of content. Perceiving the worry identified with preemptive blocking of content by mediators to not draw in possible risk, the Supreme Court read down the commitment of delegates. The court has now deciphered the expression "actual knowledge" to just incorporate court or government orders. Subsequently, the commitment to obstruct content has simply been restricted to situations where the delegate gets a court or government request. The Delhi High Court, in Super Cassettes Industries Ltd. v. Myspace Inc. and Anr[xxxiv], passed a milestone administering with connection to intermediary law. The Court expected that an intermediary may hold to take responsibility for encroaching content facilitated on its foundation just when it has explicit or real information or motivation to accept that such data might be encroaching. The addition of ads and alteration of content designs by a delegate through a computerized interaction and without manual intercession doesn't bring about the mediator being considered to have real information on the content facilitated. When an intermediary has been educated by a complainant of possibly encroaching substances facilitated on its foundation, it isn't committed to proactively confirm and eliminate content along these lines facilitated on its foundation that may encroach the protected innovation privileges of the complainant.

Anti-Money Laundering Laws

In India, the law which prevents money laundering activities is the Prevention of Money Laundering Act, 2002[xxxv] ("PMLA"). The PMLA was thus amended by the Prevention of Money Laundering (Amendment) Act 2012[xxxvi], which achieved huge changes to the consistency in systems needed under the PMLA. The PMLA requires reporting entities to keep up records of transactions and reports proving the character of their customers as per the Rules. The accompanying reports are needed to be kept up by Gaming Entities:

1. Records of the identity of the clients are required to be maintained.
2. Know Your Customer (KYC) norms and Anti-Money Laundering (AML) standards under the PMLA.
3. Recording all transactions

Indian states and their perception of gaming laws

Punjab and Haryana

Gambling is illegal in Punjab[xxxvii]. The first online lottery game was introduced in Punjab, in 2008. The Punjab Gambling Law states that betting, wager or a bet made regarding any horse, mere or gelding competition will amount to gaming. The law further states that a house, room, tent, vehicle, vessel or other place used for gaming purposes should be regarded as a common gaming house. Any article or document used as an accessory for easing gaming should be regarded as an instrument of gaming. Any person who possesses such a gaming house or gaming instrument for making a profit will be guilty. While hearing a petition filed by Advocate VarunGumber, Justice AmitRawal held that taking part in an online fantasy game requires a particular degree of skill, so it would be regarded as gambling.

Online lottery is also known as Internet gambling. During the Congress rule, it was considered illegal. The Punjab Government in 2013 approved online lottery and horse racing. Not only this, but some ministers considered Internet Gambling as a fundraising project. The Cricket Board of Punjab supported this order. The Punjab Government is now earning 30 crores from online lottery expecting to grow ten times more in the years to come.

The State of Telangana

The Government of the State of Telangana has been exceptionally sharp towards guaranteeing the restriction of betting in general, both online and offline. The Telangana Gaming (Amendment) Act, 2017[xxxviii] (hereinafter alluded to as the "Telangana Amendment Act") executes the arrangement of zero resistance against betting which genuinely affects the monetary status and prosperity of the basic public. It covers inside its ambit any demonstration of gambling cash on a dubious occasion, remembering for a game of skill.

Under the arrangements of the said Telangana Gaming Act, Rummy has been recognized not as a game of skill. The President of India has given his consent to the Telangana Prevention of Dangerous Activities of Bootleggers, Dacoits, Drug-Offenders, Goondas, Immoral Traffic Offenders and Land-Grabbers (Amendment) Bill, 2017[xxxix] (hereinafter alluded to as the "Bill") which makes culpable the demonstrations betting or wagering on games of skill like rummy.

The recently authorized Act would punish the playing of rummy on physical just as virtual media.

Gujarat Poker laws

Poker is an illegal game in Gujarat[xl]. A petition was filed by the Indian Poker Association's secretary KN Suresh and Advocate MaluinPandya. They claimed that IPA came into an agreement with YMCA Club to build poker players who can represent India at the International level. They cited state law in its petition stating that poker does not form a part of gambling and hence it will not be covered under the scope of the Gujarat Prevention of Gambling Act, 1887[xli]. Justice Sonia Gokani asked for the government's reply about the legal aspects of the popular card game.

Illegal casino raided

According to the gambling laws of Gujarat, any gaming instrument seized in any room is considered illegal. In 2014, following this law, Bangalore's Central Crime Branch (CCB) raided an illegal mobile casino. It is reported that 61 persons were detained by the police along with 70 mobiles, packets of ganja, bottles of whisky and 1977 gambling tokens.

IPL betting laws

Three cricketers were arrested by the Police under the gambling laws in India. S Sreesanth, AjitChandila and AnkeetChavan associated with the Indian Premier League were arrested from the Landmark hotel in Kanpur which was hosting the teams of Delhi Daredevils and Gujarat Lions. The investigation operation conducted by the Superintendent of Kanpur Police reported that they had seized Rs 40.90 lakh in cash and five mobile phones.

Poker and Rummy is Games of Skill

The verdict given by the Gujarat High Court on the legality of poker served as the biggest milestone in the history of gambling. The court held rummy, poker, bridge games and naps as the games of skill.

Mumbai

Casino games, video slot games etc, are banned but you can enjoy playing them online.

Gambling laws in Maharashtra

The gambling laws in Maharashtra[xlii] are operated by the Maharashtra Prevention of Gambling Act, 1887[xliii] and states that everyone should abide by the laws of the Public Gaming Act, 1867. Involved in gambling or any other activity involving profit-making is an offence and is a crime punishable by the law of Maharashtra. To own a gaming house and visit it is also illegal. Except for rummy and horseracing every other game is prohibited. Maharashtra has its turf club for organizing horse racing events within their state.

The Maharashtra Prevention of Gambling Act, 1887

According to Maharashtra's Gambling Act, Gambling is illegal in Maharashtra and punishable by law, but the laws are not stringent enough. If one is found possessing a gaming house or conducting such games or even visiting such events then he/she will be subjected to a fine of Rs 200 with imprisonment for one month as an offence committed for the first time. If one is found committing the same offence again then he/she will be subjected to a fine of Rs 200 and imprisonment for 3 months. If one is found to be committing such an offence for the third time then he/she will be imprisoned for 6 months with no fine.

Sports Betting in Maharashtra

Football, tennis, soccer, kabaddiand IPL games are banned in Maharashtra except rummy and horse racing. But people still bet on international betting sites particularly made for Indian payers as Indian law is not allowed to intervene on foreign sites.

Horse Racing in Maharashtra

Horse racing is one of the few legal games that follows the Bombay Race Courses Licencing Act, 1912 and is considered a game of skill followed by the investment of the people. One has to pay 30.90% tax from their winning amount as per Section 115B of the Income Tax Act, 1961. Status on Card Games: Rummy, Poker, Flush etc.

An order passed by the Supreme Court held that playing poker and rummy falls under the list of skill-based games and hence one can play it with their friends and family at home. But it is illegal to play these games in real money clubs or official gaming houses.

The Mahalakshmi Saga: online gaming

This case was a challenge by the Mahalakshmi Cultural Association before the Supreme Court against the impugned order passed by the Madras High Court in the case of Satyanarayana Case(State of Andhra Pradesh v Satyanarayana)[xliv] with relation to the Rummy played in brick and mortar clubs. The background of the case is that the Inspector of the Chennai Police raided the place of the Mahalakshmi Cultural Association because the place was being used for gambling and that the members were playing rummy with stakes and the case was filed against the Association. A writ petition was filed before a single Judge by the association to seek directions forbidding the police from inter alia interfering with the activities being conducted by the association in matters regarding the playing of 13 cards games of rummy with or without stakes. The Court disposed of the writ petition in the favour of the Association on the reason that the rummy is a skill-based game and hence not illegal. This decree passed by the single judge was challenged by the police officials stating that the Madras High Court in the Satyanarayana Case held that if a club or an association allows its members or guests to play rummy with stakes and make a profit out of such play then the police has the power to invoke the Chennai City Police Act. While the SC was heading with the proceeding of the Mahalakshmi Case, an intervention application was filed by Games 24x7 and by Rummy websites pleading for clarification of the order passed by the Madras High Court for the legality of online rummy since their business was getting affected as the banks refused to process payments to the players on this site and also the physical rummy providers had a fear of criminal prosecution. The Supreme Court held that the Impugned Order passed by the Madras High Court did not deal with online Rummy and it will be applied only on the Rummy played in bricks and mortar clubs. Moreover, the Court noted that the State has not yet decided as to whether or not the provision of online Rummy would constitute gambling under the Chennai City Police Act, so the Court did not feel it important to entertain the plea related to the legality of online gaming. Strikingly, the Supreme Court has not yet convincingly managed the legality of online gaming.

Although, it was expected that the Supreme Court will lie down the law related to what business models (including online) would amount to gambling as restricted under the State Gambling legislations yet the matter remains grey.

<u>Bombay High Court's observation in the case of Dream 11</u>

In 2017, the High Court of Punjab and Haryana in the case of Shri Varun Gumber v Union of India and Ors[xlv] held that Dream11 is a skill-based online fantasy sport and playing it does not equal gambling. Dream 11 is a fantasy sports platform based in India that allows users to play fantasy hockey, cricket, kabaddi, football and basketball. The Punjab and Haryana High Court held that no betting or gambling is involved in the fantasy game employed by Dream11 and the result is not dependent upon winning or losing of any particular team in the real world on any given day. A Criminal Public Interest Litigation (PIL) was filed against Dream11 before the Bombay High Court. The PIL claimed that Dream11 was carrying out illegal functioning of gambling/betting/wagering in the guise of Online Fantasy Sports Gaming ("OFSG") and hence should be punished under the Public Gambling Act, 1867 ("Act"). The PIL then claimed that Dream11 breached the Central Goods and Service Tax Act, 2017 ("CGST Act")[xlvi] read with Rule 31A of Central Goods and Service Tax Rules, 2018 ("CGST Rules' ')[xlvii].

The Bombay High Court in this case agreed with the decision of Punjab and Haryana High Court and held that the games played on the Dream 11 platform were games of skill and not games of chance. The court held that if the consequence of the game is set merely by chance or accident, any money put on stake with the cognizance of risk and desire to gain would be 'gambling' or 'betting'. Since that is not the situation of fantasy games played on the Dream 11 platform, the same does not amount to gambling or betting. It held that just if their OFSG is 'gambling' or 'betting', there is an extension to deduce the possibility of any tax evasion. It further decided that the sums pooled by the players in the security account are an 'actionable claim' as the equivalent is to be dispersed among the winning participants according to the result of the game. OFSG on Dream 11's platform is not like betting or gambling, the High Court decided that money pooled by the players cannot be exposed to GST.

Suggestions to the existing legislations

It is suggested[xlviii] to introduce a gambling tax similar to the application of luxury tax as it can provide a higher tax revenue collection that will safeguard the economically vulnerable from falling into prey.

To protect the economic and social interests of minors, a law must be introduced to prohibit minors from placing bets.

The establishment of a gambling association is just as it is responsible for the regulation and administration of bets. Registration must be made mandatory and the commission must allow licenses on analyzing the source and flow of money placed in the transaction and the tax paid before allowing licenses. It will keep a check on illegal gambling in India, hence, giving protection to the bettors who fall prey to bookies.

In the constitutional context, it is significant to amend the Gambling Act, of 1867 to incorporate 'authorized games' on which bets can be set if it is taxed and transaction enlisted. Right now, the Gambling Act precludes betting yet this does not apply to 'Games off skills' exposing the horseracing-cricket legislative distinction. Consequently, there is a need to part with the current characterization and set up an approved list of sports that bets can be put upon.

All the guidelines must be illustrated under entry 42 of the Union list that deals with interstate trade and commerce to protect the business interests of the parties involved in betting.

The Information Technology Act, 2000 should expand to direct online sports betting transactions and their legitimacy vis-à-vis the Constitution. To help this, Entry 31 of the union list relating to phones and different methods of broadcasting and communication should be altered to chalk out administrative instruments, for example, tracking the age of the bettor online, requesting a tax return from online betting transactions to guarantee the appropriateness of the IT Act successfully

The central government should likewise assume the liability of forcing implicit rules, practices and techniques alongside making authorizing brokers compulsory. Such licenses should be repudiated on the non-installment of taxes or illegal exchange of the cash placed in cash, particularly to terrorist or mafia associations.

To advance games that are not in the commercial spotlight, the Government can restrict the sum put down on bets of a specific game, along these lines guiding wagers to be put on sports that have recently been disregarded. This can activate those games that need the monetary help and consolation recently repudiated.

Conclusion

Internet Gaming is a multi-crore industry in India. Notwithstanding this reality, we have no devoted Online Gaming and Online Gambling Laws in India. This has made the Legal Position in regards to Online Games like Rummy, Poker, and so on truly befuddling and cloudy. Because of assorted legitimate activities and circumstances, the matter has reached under the steady gaze of the Supreme Court of India. Notwithstanding, there are incredibly mistaken assumptions and misguided judgments in regards to the idea of present legitimate procedures under the steady gaze of the Indian Supreme Court.

For example, the centre issue under the watchful eye of the Supreme Court relates to the Legality of playing Rummy with Cash Stakes. The Supreme Court for this situation isn't worried about Online Rummy and it is certainly not worried about Online Poker, Supreme Court has completely referenced that it would not choose the legitimacy of online poker or online rummy till the Indian government comes out with an approach choice in such a manner. Before, the Supreme Court requested that the Indian government explain its stand concerning online rummy however the public authority wouldn't give any assessment in such a manner. Accordingly, the lawfulness of online poker or online rummy is as yet an ill-defined situation and online gaming and betting partners should conform to the relevant laws of India till the Indian government comes up with some strategy or law in such a manner.

The situation on a date is that online games sites in India are now in an in-between state and now the Supreme Court of India has made this position unsure and lawfully powerless. According to the most recent request of the Supreme Court, it has wouldn't choose the legitimateness or illicitness of online games like poker, rummy, and so forth The Supreme Court has explained that the current petitions before it relate to offline rummy just and overseeing on the online rummy or online poker is as yet a legitimately unsafe territory.

Presently the ball is in the Indian government's court and it needs to think of rules and guidelines in regards to internet games and web-based betting exercises in India. The Indian government needs to choose about the skills as opposed to betting rules as well as the techno lawful viewpoints that are owing to utilization of innovation in online gaming.

Author's Biography

This article is written by Sabaat Fatima from School of Law, HILSR, Jamia Hamdard. This is an exhaustive article that will give you a brief knowledge about the present legal framework of the gaming laws in India and the demand for implementing a separate legal framework for online gambling.

CHAPTER TWENTY-FOUR

LEGISLATIVE RELATIONS

Author: Aryan Sinha, IV year of B.B.A.,LL.B.(Hons.) from Galgotias University

Introduction

Indian Constitution provides a new kind of federalism called as quasi-federalism to cover the Indian situation. India is declared as "Union of States"[i]. A federal system divides Indian polity into two parts; Union and State. When government organizes Union of States under Central government rather than separate individual State, such kind of organization is called as quasi-federalism[ii].

The legislative relation between Union and State are mentioned into "Article 245 to Article 255 under Part XI of the Constitution of India"[iii]. In fact, Legislative relation between Union and States are subject to distribution of power between three lists as provided under schedule 7 mentioned in Indian Constitution.

The Constitution of India divides the legislative powersinto two parts-

1. Territorial Legislative Jurisdiction
2. Legislative Subject Matter

Territorial Legislative Jurisdiction

"Extent of laws made by Parliament and by the Legislature of States"[iv].

Article 245 provides the territorial extent of legislative power of Union and State. Clause 1 provides wider power to Parliament than the State Legislature. It says Parliament may make law for the any part or whole of India subject to the Constitutional provisions. Clause 2 provides extra-territorial legislation. It gives one general rule that Parliament may make law extra-territorial but State may not make law extra-territorial. There is one exception to the above mentioned general rule where State Legislature has also power to legislate beyond the territorial limit of its State only in the condition where Constitutional provisions permits to legislature and there is direct relation between the legislative State and subject matter. Union Parliamentary laws may extend its enforceability outside India. .

Legislative Subject Matter

Subject Matter of Laws Made by Parliament and by the Legislature of States Under Article 246

There are three lists for distribution of power-

- Union List: It contains subject matter of national interest. For example; Defense, CBI, Investigation, Atomic energy, War, Space, banking , foreign affairs, Airways, RBI, Taxes, Currency etc.
- State List: It contains subject matter of State or local interest. For example; State public order, State police and State officers and State High courts, health etc.
- The Concurrent List: It contains with respect to legislation power of both.

The subject matter of Concurrent list makes legislation procedure flexible in nature and made this procedure quasi-federal in nature. It contains general and social welfare subject matter. State or Union Parliament can take any initiative accordingly.

Article 246 Deals With Subject-Matter of Laws Made by Parliament and by The Legislatures of States

Doctrine of Interpretation of Subject Matter under Article 246

1. Doctrine of Harmonious Construction

The aim and objective of this doctrine are to avoid overriding effects of legislative provisions in one particular subject to make all effective. It is a balancing interpretation of the specific so that none of the legislation becomes ineffective as well as the conflict between two legislative provisions within the same Legislation does not arise.[v]

2. Doctrine of Pith and Substance

As the name suggests, the meaning of this doctrine is to check the essential and true nature of the subject matter. The literal meaning of the word "pith" is true nature and "Substance" is essential. This doctrine is applicable in such situations where there is a conflict between provisions of Legislation. In that case, the interpretation of the Legislation will be done according to the law as a whole, not on its separate or Independent provisions. Any kind of legislation which is in general within the competence of legislator would be considered as Constitutional even though it may in some situations appears beyond the competency of legislature due to the interpretation of that legislation according to the doctrine of pith and substance.There is one case of Prafulla Kumar Mukherjee v. Bank of Commerce[vi] in whichthe judgment provides the wider meaning of the doctrine.

Aspect theory

Aspect theory originates its roots from Canada. In Lefroy's Canada's Federal System[vii], the learned Author referred to the "aspects of legislation". When legislature subject falls within another legislative power", the learned Author says:"... that by 'aspect' must be understood the aspect or point of view of the legislator in legislating the object, purpose, and scope of the legislation that the word is used subjectively of the legislator, rather than objectively of the matter legislated upon."

In India, general meaning of aspect theory –

There is a division of power in the Indian Constitution and there may be a situation where one subject is common between two lists. Such kind overlapping of subject matter is considered as valid law according to aspect theory.

Role of Judiciary and Aspect theory

Indian judiciary plays an important role in the growth of aspect theory. In case of Tata sky Ltd. V. State of Punjab[viii], there were many judicial decisions discussed in this case in relation to aspect theory. Reference was made to following observation in Federation of hotel & restaurant assn. of India v. Union of India[ix], the Supreme Court observed that: "The subject matter of case was contended as conflict issue. It was expenditure tax under central tax under list I & simultaneously as substance tax under central tax under entry 62 of list II. A legislation like Finance Act can be supported on the basis of a number of entries. In the present case, we are concerned with the Constitutional status of the levy, namely, service tax. The nomenclature of a levy is not conclusive for deciding its true nature & particular levy with reference to the legislative competence, the court has to look into the pith and substance of the legislation, the powers of Parliament & State legislatures are subject to Constitutional limitations. Tax laws are governed by part XII & XIII. "Article 265"[x] takes in A. 245 when it says that the tax shall be levied by the authority of law.After referring to judgments in "Gujrat Ambuja Cements Ltd. V. UOI"[xi], "T.N Kalyana Mandapam Assn.

v. UOI"[xii], "International Tourists Corpn. V. State of Haryana"[xiii], with the above-mentioned observations, the theory of aspect is concluded.

3. The Doctrine of Colorable Legislation

The rule interpretation of legislation is entirely opposite to the doctrine of pith and substance. Under this doctrine, the legislator enacts law out of its competence but forcefully gives different-different colors to show or prove it within its competence, in such situation, the law would be considered as invalid and different colors will not be able to protect its validity.

Residuary Powers of Legislation

These powers are generally called as last resort. When there is any subject matter which is directly or indirectly does not fall into any of the three lists, then such powers are exercised by Parliament. "Article 248"[xiv], Union list 1 entry 97 says that for any other matter not enumerated in List II and List III including any tax or not mentioned in either of those lists,

Parliament Power to Legislate on State Subject

"These powers of parliament to legislate are discussed below in details as follow

1. Legislation for National interest(Article 249)
2. Legislation during an emergency (Article 250)
3. Legislation with consent of States (Article 252)
4. Legislation for giving effect to an international agreement (Article 253)
5. Legislation after failure of Constitutional machinery in State"[xv]

Conclusion

The aim or objective of federal system for division or distribution of power or authority between federal government & the State is mentioned in schedule 7, list 3. There is division of legislative & administrative powers between the Union & State government and the Supreme Court stands at the head of our judiciary to jealously guard this distribution of powers & to invalidate any action which violates the limitation imposed by the Constitution. There are some provisions given by Indian Constitution, where Centre has supremacy

Additions Made

Quasi Federal would mean a unitary state with subsidiary federal features. Another scholar CH Alexandrowicz has raised the question of whether India should at all be called a federal state?[xvi]

Pre-World War-II, federalism was regarded as a model in which several autonomous units came together. But this conception is getting outdated. Indian model of federalism is based on modern understanding, according to which only a strong Union can keep the Country together and is necessary for the conditions in which the Constitution is operating.

CHAPTER TWENTY-FIVE

EXPANDING HORIZONS OF EQUALITY

Author: Pavitra Balgi, III year of B.B.A.,LL.B.(Hons.) from Amity University, Mumbai

INTRODUCTION

Equality is the state of being equal without discrimination and impartiality and biasness. It a status conferred upon individuals wherein their gender , social status , economical status, race , religion is not taken into consideration. All humans are of the same status, there is no inferior or superior person. In equality not treating everyone in the same way , but it is a process, if in which a person is put through the end result or outcome would be same and equal for all. This process might be different for different but the end result will always be the same.

The rights dealing with equality are given from Article 14 to Article 18 in the Indian Constitution. Article 14 of the Indian Constitution:- Equality before the law and equal protection before the law.

This right was originally considered as a negative right of a person since it includes that one should not be discriminated with respect to public offices or public places. A negative right basically meaning giving freedom to an individual to do or not to do some action. For example one should not be restricted due to gender for accessing a public park. This was the original concept of equality which did not take into consideration the other aspects of inequality. Article 14 is conferred upon everyone be it a citizen or a non-citizen. The equality before law and equal protection of law is for all within the territory in India.

In [1]State of West Bengal v. Anwar Ali Sarkar,, Chief Justice Patanjali Shastri had quoted that , there cannot be any violation of law in absence of equal protection before the law. However the courts have concluded that there is nothing much common between them. The term law " Equality before law" means that everybody will be treated the same when an law is applied whereas law in " Equal protection of Laws" mean specific laws made for specific individuals. Various jurists have also said that the concept of equality in dynamic and ever changing in nature.

The application of this article is for the all the natural persons iemale , female and also transgenders. Article 14 does not discrimination against any person sexual identity and orientation.

Principle behind Article 14

No two individuals are the same is a known fact other than belonging to the homo sapiens. Comparison between individuals can only be done when both the individuals are at the same position or of same status. When comparison is done between individuals of different status or financial position etc , it gives rise to inequality. The main propagation by this article is that there should be equality between the equals. Comparison between purchasing power of a person with salary of Rs 10,000 per month and purchasing power of a person with salary of Rs 1,00,000 cannot be said to be equal since one will spend with accordance to his income. Article 14 suggests that there is no uniformity in equality , to attain equality, comparison has to be done between equals. There is a differentiation which must be done between the equals and un-equals.

Legislative classification

Since the principle of equality means that comparison must be done amongst equals and not un-equals , from this it can be concluded safely that it doesn't mean universal application of law. It can be derived that the application of certain laws require one to fit in the particular category in which it is dealing with. For example laws related to lawyers with respect to their code of conduct and their qualification cannot be applicable to doctors. It is necessary for such classification to be made. Different laws are applicable to different classes of people for the purpose of public welfare. In the case of [2] Kedar Nath Bajoria v. State of West Bengal , the Supreme Court held that equal protection doesn't mean same laws should be applied to everyone , it means laws are classified with accordance to people, their profession etc and also that the State doesn't have any authority to classify for the purpose of legislation.

Reasonable classification

The legislative classification made must be reasonable and should have proper substance with regards to the classification made, without reason if some classification is made them it will be deemed to be arbitrary and increase the inequality between masses. There are two conditions which must be satisfied while making such classifications

1. Classification on the basis of intelligible differentia
2. The relation with the differentia made and statute must be rationale

For example in Indian Contract Act , section 11 specifies that minor cannot enter into contract, in this case the differentia is made on the basis of age. The reason being the minor does not have the capacity to give consent. So there are two groups made ie minors and majors with respect to age to enter into a contract

3. The classification must be lawful and in good faith.

The article 14 allows the classification or bifurcation but disregards and disallows the classes created by legislation. The article suggests that the laws may not be general or the same law shall be applicable irrespective of the circumstance or situation. There is no uniformity in it. The people belonging to the classes made should be treated in the same way. These classifications are also made with the view of protecting and regulating the state affairs. Therefore the classification according to this article should be reasonable and not vague.

Provisions regarding women , children , scheduled caste and scheduled tribes

The article 14 considered everybody equal before the law . But nothing stops or restricts the State to make laws or provisions with respect to women , children , scheduled caste and scheduled tribes.

For example the section 497 of Indian Penal Code suggests that the offence of adultery can be committed only by men and not women. With consideration to the women's status in the society , the law was clearly made by the state for women and is justified.

In the case of [3]State of madras v. Champakamdorairajan, there were certain seats in the medical and engineeering colleges reserved for students belonging to the some particular community. The court held that the particular classification is not justified since it was making classification on the basis of some caste or religion. After this case the clause 4 of article 15 was inserted which confers the government to prepare certain provisions for the people of social and economic backward classes for their enrichment in the fields of education and also the scheduled tribes and scheduled tribes.

Expanding horizons of equality

In the case of [4]E.PRoyappa v. state of Tamil Nadu, the judges said that equality is a very dynamic and ever changing concept which cannot be subdued for restricted from growing. It is conferred upon the citizen to protect them against the arbitrary actions and decisions of the state. This is the rudimentary principle of equality.

In the case of [5]Maneka Gandhi v. Union of India, the judges regarding the procedures established by law said that article 14 is given to control arbitrary actions of the state and make sure that everyone is treated equally and fairly. The principle of reasonableness is also equally essential in such cases.

CONCLUSION

There are multiple of cases which show the expanding horizons and interpretations of the term equality under article 14. The term equality is now not only restricted to its generic meaning of being equal. It has also evolved and is applicable under various circumstance and will continue growing with the modernisation

CHAPTER TWENTY-SIX

THE EVOLUTION OF ECO-CENTRIC WORLD IN THE AFTERMATH OF COVID – 19

Author: Aleena Rose Jose, III year of B.Com.,LL.B.(Hons.) from His Highness Maharajas Govt. Law College, Ernakulam

Introduction

Homi J Bhabha who is enthroned in the minds of millions of Indians as the mastermind behind the success of atomic energy in India was also a great visionary who taught us how to carry on the developmental projects without harming the nature.

One day as Bhabha was travelling by a car to his office, he heard the noise of cutting trees. He asked his driver to stop the car and came out. There he saw a few workers chopping the branches of a tree in order to cut it down. Bhabha asked them, 'Why are you cutting the tree?' They starred at him and replied "We are doing this as per the instruction of the municipal engineer. We must do it for broadening the road. See, this tree is in the middle of the road". Bhabha pleaded them to stop their work for an hour. They agreed. He hastly got into the car. As soon as he reached the office he called Vaidya, the head of landscaping in the Atomic Research Centre and discussed with him how to save the tree. Vaidya headed to the Peddar Road in Bombay where he saw the men waiting for him. Under the supervision of Vaidya the workmen plucked off the tree without damaging its main root. With the help of a crane it was replanted carefully in a pit dug nearby. Bhabha thanked Vaidya and said that he was so delighted as the could save the tree. Spreading its branches around, that rain tree is still alive as a homage to the great scientist.

When we think about an eco-centric world, the first and foremost challenge is to strike a balance between development and nature conservation. The above incident is very relevant in the current scenario where people started to think about an eco centric lifestyle amidst of Covid-19. Development and nature conservation are inevitable factors of our existence and should go hand in hand. No one is too small to make a difference. A difference is made when we give nature a voice in our decision making.

Eco-centric Worldview

A shift from anthropocentric worldview to eco centric worldview is essential for solving the environmental crisis. Ecocentrism finds inherent value in all of nature. It takes a much wider view of the world than does anthropocentrism . Ecocentrism is the broadest of world views but there are related worldviews. Ecocentrism goes beyond biocentrism by including environmental systems as whole and their abiotic aspects. I t also goes beyond zoo-centrism on account of explicitly including flora and ecological contexts of organisms. Ecocentrism is thus the umbrella that includes biocentrism and zoo-centrism because all these worldviews values the non-human, with ecocentrism having the widest vision. Given that life relies on geological processes and geomorphology to sustain it, and that 'geodiversity' also has intrinsic value, the broader term 'ecocentrism' seems most appropriate. Ecocentrism as a worldview has been with humanity since we evolved. It can be defined as a value shift fromHomo sapiensto planet earth.1

Will Covid-19 have a Lasting Impact on the Environment?

A look at the statistics gives us an idea about the changes Covid-19 have brought to our ecosystem and how can it contribute to the evolution of an eco-centric world.

Covid-19 was declared as a global pandemic by WHO on 11th March 2020. The world came to a standstill with an unexpected shutdown of everyday activities. The streets of Wuhan, China are deserted after authorities implemented a strict lockdown. In London, the normally bustling pubs, bars and theatres have been closed and people have been told to stay in their homes. Worldwide, flights are being cancelled or turning around in the mid air, as the aviation industry buckles. Those who are able to do so are holed up at home, practicing social distancing and working remotely.It all aimed at controlling the spread of Covid-19 and hopefully reducing the death toll. But all these changes has also led to some unexpected consequences.

Positive Environmental Impacts

Restricted human interaction with nature during crisis time has appeared as a blessing for nature and environment. As industries, transport networks and businesses have closed down, it has brought a sudden drop in carbon emissions. Compared with 2019, levels of pollution in NewYork have reduced nearly 50% in 2020 because of measures to contain virus.

In China, emissions felt 25% at the start of 2020 as people were instructed to stay at home, factories shuttered and coal use fell by 40% at China's 6 largest power plants since the last quarter of 2019. The proportion of days with 'good quality air' was up 11.4% compared with the year before pandemic in 337 cities across China, according to its Ministry of Ecology and Environment. In Europe, satellite images show nitrogen dioxide emissions fading away over Northern Italy. A similar story is playing out in Spain, India and the UK. In Venice, water in the canal cleared and experienced greater water flow. According to German scientist Rainer Froese, the fish biomass will increase due to sharp decline in fishing. As people stayed home due to lockdown and travel restrictions, some animals have been spotted in cities. Sea turtles were spotted laying eggs on beaches they once avoided. In USA, fatal vehicle collisions with animals such as deer, elk, moose, bears, mountain lions fell by 58% during March and April 2020.[2]

Only an immediate and essential threat like Covid-19 would have led to such a profound change so fast, at the time of writing, global deaths from the virus had passed 56 lakhs with more than 37 crore cases confirmed worldwide.[3] As well as the toll of early deaths, the pandemic has brought widespread job losses and threatened the livelihoods of millions as businesses struggle to cope up with the restrictions being put in place to control the virus. Economic activities has stalled and stock markets have tumbled alongside the falling carbon emissions. It's the precisely opposite to the drive towards a decarbonized sustainable economy that many have been advocating for decades.

A pandemic that is claiming people's lives should not be seen as a way of bringing about environment change either. Eventhough we can say that this may contribute to evolution of an eco- centric world, for one thing, its far from certain how lasting this dip in emissions will be. When the pandemic eventually subsides, will carbon and pollutant emissions 'bounce back' so much that it will be as if this clear skied interlude never happened? Or could the changes we see today have a more persistent effect. We cannot answer this crucial question with a complete yes or no.

According to Kimberly Nicholas, a sustainability science researcher at Lund University in Sweden, the first thing to be considered is the different reasons that emissions dropped. If we take transport for example which makeup 23% of global carbon emissions. These emissions have fallen in short terms in the countries where public health measures such as keeping people in their home, have cut unnecessary travel. Driving and aviation are key contributors to emissions from transport contributing to 72% and 11% of the transport sectors greenhouse gas emissions respectively. We know that for the duration of reduced travel during the pandemic, these emissions will stay lowered. But what will happen when measures are eventually lifted? In terms of routine trips like commuting, those miles left untraveled during the pandemic are not going to comeback – you are not going to travel today to make up for all the times you worked from home, says Nicholas. But what about other kinds of travel-might the cabin fever of self isolation encourage people to travel more when the option is there again.4

On the other hand, it may be the care that people who are avoiding travel right now are really appreciating spending time with their families and focusing on those really core priorities. These moments of crisis can highlight how important those priorities and help people focus on the health and wellbeing of family, friends and community. If this changes in focus as a result of the pandemic sticks, then this could help to keep emissions lower. But there is another way it could go. It could also be that people are putting of long distance trips but plan on taking them later. Frequently flying forms a large part of carbon footprint for people who do it regularly. So, these emissions could simply comeback if people return to their old habits. The positive environmental effects of Covid-19 reduction of noise pollution, ecological restoration and assimilation of tourist spots.

<u>Negative Environmental Impacts</u>

Other than positive impacts Covid-19 bought to our ecosystem, medical waste management has became a challenging issue. Some people are at high risk of adverse effects from contact to medical wastes as well, including cleaners, trash collectors and some other people who have to spend a great amount of time in public places.

The masks we use are made up of plastic based materials that are liquid-resistant and are long lasting after they are discarded, ending up in ocean or landfill. The surgical masks should not be worn longer than one day, discarding them and empty bottles of hand sanitizer along with solid tissue papers are ending up to a huge trail of medical waste in the environment. For instance, an environmental NGO- Oceans Asia in Soko islands took a survey, according to it, in HonKong, were Covid-19 infection started in January 2020, a large amount of discarded single-use masks washed upto a 100 metre stretch of beach. Due to the Covid-19 outbreak, the general public have started wearing surgical measures. When 7 million people suddenly start wearing one or a couple of masks daily, single use gloves and hand sanitizers, the amount of trash created is going to be substantial. The contrary impacts of such medical wastes are far reaching. When these are remained discarded in an animals natural habitat in both land and ocean this could cause animals to mistakenly eat this as food and lead in their deaths.5

This is not the first time an epidemic has left its mark on atmospheric CO2 levels. Throughout history, the spread of disease has been linked to lower emissions-even well before the industrial age. It is found that epidemics such as the Black Death in Europe in the 14th century and the diseases such as smallpox brought to South America with the arrival of Spanish conquistadors in the 16th century, both left subtle marks on atmospheric CO2 levels. The impact from today's outbreak is not predicted to lead to anywhere near the death tolls of these pandemics, it is unlikely to lead to widespread change of land use. Its environmental impacts are more akin to those of recent world events, such as the financial crash of 2008 and 2009. Then, global emissions dropped immensely for an year. Eventhough the financial crash of 2008-09 led to an overall dip in emissions, but this quickly rebounded by 2010 as the economy recovered, leading to an all time high. There are hints that corona virus will act the same way. One of the factor that could influence whether or not these emissions bounce back is how long the corona pandemic lasts. At the moment it is hard to predict. But, it could be that we see longer term and more substantial effects. If the corona virus outbreak continues long then consumer demand could remain low because of low wages.

According to researchers such as Glen Peters of the Centre for International Climate and Environment Research in Ohio have noted that overall 2020 may still see a drop in global emissions of 0.3% less pronounced than the crash of 2008-09, but also with an opportunity for less rebound if efforts to stimulate the economy are focused towards sectors such as clean energy.

From the above studies we can almost arrive at a conclusion that Covid -19 can't bring about a long term impact in our environment as situation rebounces when the virus eventually subsides. But it is clear that if there is limited human intervention, the nature makes use of its cleansing power to clear out the water bodies and atmosphere and its we who should give a chance.

Eventhough Covid-19 alone can't lead to the evolution of an eco -centric world, we can use this as the first step towards attaining the goal. If we succeed in keeping our environment to an extent as if it is now, then we are a step nearer to the target. If we are able to contribute certain other factors to the present ecological impacts caused by Covid-19, an eco- centric world will be evolved in the near future.

What can we do?

'No One is Too Small to Make a Difference' is a collection of Greta Thunberg's climate action speeches. The title must be taken to heart by all. She is a 9th grade student who made a difference. She started the activism from home. She challenged her parents to lower the family's carbon footprint and overall impact on environment by becoming vegan, upcycling and giving up flying. This is the first step, change should be initiated by ourselves in our families.

According to Greta, "People are suffering. People are dying. Entire ecosystems are collapsing We are at the beginning of a mass extinction. And all you can talk about is money and fairy tales of eternal economic growth. How dare you?"6 Egocentric leadership is the root cause of our environmental crisis. We must change the way we understand and relate to the natural world. To do so, cultivate an eco-centric not egocentric mindset. Our planet is in trouble. Evenafter mobilizing millions of dollars to mitigate and respond to the damaging effects of climate change, we may only addressing the symptoms of a deep rooted issue. We have seen a significant rise in declarations of climate emergency, conferences, coalitions and innovations to address climate change- but we are also seeing an increasing gap between what is needed and what is actually been done to safeguard our planet. Coming forward and signing international contracts relating to environmental crisis and withdrawing from them before the tenure is completed can be regarded as utter cowardness.

Today's dominant leadership is egocentric. Our planet needs eco-centric leadership. For the evolution of an eco-centric world we need eco-centric leaders who truly embody empathy, walk the talk and demonstrate the courage needed to create a better green world.

Eco-centrism has been labelled 'anti-human' or as contrary to concerns for social justice. This is not true as an ecocentrist overwhelmingly support inter human social justice. However they also support interspecies justice or ecojustice, for the non-human world. Just as environmental systems evolve many interrelationships, environmental and social systems are entwined and so social and ecojustice.

Therefore, social wellbeing is essential for the evolution of an eco-centric world. Wars, bombs, terrorism and internal conflicts hampers it. Displacement of people due to war and riots affects the nature effectively. The flow of refugees should be an issue of concern. A society where male and female live happily and peacefully by equally sharing their responsibilities is essential for the attainment of an eco-centric world. War and use of nuclear weapons must be strictly monitored. It can cause huge damage to life and property of humans and a huge destruction of flora and fauna. The radiations emitted may last for centuries. Maintaining peace and harmony in the frontiers and friendly relationship with neibouring countries is essential.

Sustainable development is vital in the evolution of an eco-centric world. A development that meets of present without compromising the needs of future generations. This concept is praised by many scholars, leaders and scientists over the time.

The Sustainable Development Goals (SDGs), set in 2015 by UN General Assembly are a collection of 17 global goals designed to be a 'blueprint to achieve a better and more sustainable future for all' and intended to be achieved by 2030.7The 17 goals are broad and interdependent. Each of the SDGs has a list of targets which are measured with indicators. Let's hope that positive environmental impacts of Covid-19 help in achieving the SDGs.

Rather than reducing the usage of vehicles we must think of switching over to alternative means. India being a subtropical country have abundance of sunlight throughout the year(except a few months). If we effectively utilize this renewable resource, in the era of electronic vehicles it can contribute a lot of sustainable development. As the photovoltaic technology which converts solar energy into electric energy is highly expensive, government can provide it in a subsidy rate. We must maximum make use of the renewable resources available in our country. Government can encourage traditional agricultural practices and dairy farming.

Conclusion

Never let anymore catastrophes claiming people's life to make us realize the importance of nature conservation. Always lend your ears to the expert opinions. Words by Dr. Madhav Gadgil a few years ago is still echoing in our ears, "Things are getting worse in Western Ghats. If delays is caused any longer to prevent it, Kerala is going to face a huge disaster. As you think this will never take millions of years to happen, it will happen within four or five years. When it happens we all will be here alive. Then you will realize who is lying".8

The biggest lesson is to learn from our mistakes and the incidents all around warns us to change our lifestyle. We must shift the way we view and relate to nature, and understand that it is a single living organism which is inextricably interconnected. We must adopt an eco-centric mindset whereby we are grateful to and revere nature, rather than considering ourselves superior to it. We must discard our transactional attitudes and cultivate a personal relationship with nature recognizing that the health and prosperity and our economy is dependent on the natural world. This way of living is not new. It is found in many ancient philosophies, religions and indigenous cultures.

We must embody these values and shift our focus from "What can nature do for me?" to "What can I do for nature?" Let these changes begin at home, from the grassroot level. Hope the upcoming COP-27 put forward some effective steps in this regard.

Greta sys, " I want to feel safe. How can I feel safe when I know we are in the greatest crisis in human history".9 The positive changes that occurred during Covid-19 will not last long if we are not serious in its implementation. Let the coming generations do not blame us in destroying this heavenly ecosystem. Covid-19 reminds us it is the high time to think about our mother earth and to choose the righteous path that we must walk through.

CHAPTER TWENTY-SEVEN

ECONOMIC IMPACT OF DISASTERS

Author: Navya P, V year of B.A.,LL.B.(Hons.) from Damodaram Sanjivayya National Law University (DSNLU)

ABSTRACT

Natural calamities are indispensable events that occur periodically across the globe. Globalization and industrialization impacted the environment severely that increased the risk of disasters. Risk reduction is one of the main objectives of Disaster Management. As per the "United Nations Report" in 20 years i.e. 1998- 2017 the economic loss caused to India due to natural disasters was USD 79.5 Billion. The economic aspect is given primary importance as all sufferings results in or is interrelated to economic loss. Economic assessments are done to understand the damage that occurred through property, infrastructure and others. The urban or smart cities such as Chennai, Bengaluru and others are also impacted due to these disasters that increase the risk of high economic loss. The burden falls upon the state that takes up the responsibility of Disaster Management. Measurement of economic loss helps to take up strategic action by authorities at times of disaster. In this article, the information on the economic loss caused due to natural disasters is collected and analyzed along with case laws. The effect on different sections of society is observed. The scope is restricted to natural disasters with a specific focus on cyclones, landslides and heavy rains. The official documents, journal articles and authorized materials are referred to.

Keywords: Natural Disasters, Cyclone, Landslides, Economic loss

"Sometimes it takes a natural disaster to reveal a social disaster"- Jim Wallis

INTRODUCTION

Indian Subcontinent with a coastline of 8000 kilometres frequently exposes to Cyclones and heavy rains on a seasonal/ periodical basis. The geographical position is considered one of the main reasons for vulnerability towards natural disasters.[1] The study conducted by Kahn showed that in comparison to African countries Asian states are prone to natural disasters 28.5 % more than it.[2]As per Global Climate Risk Index Report published in the year 2019, India stands at 14th vulnerable country to weather-related events. In terms of economic loss, the country ranked at 4th which recorded a loss of $13,789 million.[3] Among all the natural disasters 30 percent constitute cyclones, heavy rains and landslides of 10 percent. Hence, cyclones, heavy rains and landslides cause a major impact on India.

Cyclones occur twice a year caused due to disturbances in the atmosphere such as air circulation. These are also associated with bad weather and storms that increases the risk of vulnerability.[4]As per the United Nations Report in 20 years i.e. 1998 – 2017 the economic loss caused to India due to natural disasters was USD 79.5 Billion.[5]The recent cyclone Amphan resulted in $14 Billion loss to India making it the costliest cyclone ever that occurred in the Indian Ocean.[6] The heavy rains can be observed in smart cities such as Chennai, Bengaluru, Mumbai and others. This is a new phenomenon that can be observed due to climate change. Landslides take place simultaneously It increased the effect on the economy in addition to the Covid-19. In the first phase of the 2021 year, the country witnessed cyclone Tauktae, Yaas, Gulab that impacted the country. Despite legislations, administrative bodies and institutional mechanisms on letter lack of proper implementation affected the country. The economic impact of these disasters varies at each stage.

BACKGROUND

Section 2(d) of the Disaster Management Act, 2005 Disaster is defined as " a catastrophe, mishap, calamity or grave occurrence in any area, arising from natural or man-made causes, or by accident or negligence which results in substantial loss of life or human suffering or damage to, and destruction of, property, or damage to, or degradation of, environment, and is of such a nature or magnitude as to be beyond the coping capacity of the community of the affected area".[7] As per the definition disasters, heavy rains and landslides are also disasters. India is regularly vulnerable to tropical cyclones. Heavy rains are a recent phenomenon that can be observed in urban cities claimed to be the result of climate change. These are rather termed as "Floods" and Urban floods. Landslides are associated with cyclones and heavy rains as they result in wind force in hilly regions. These occur frequently in India among all other natural disasters.

The Disaster Management Act, 2005 provides a legal framework for the management of disasters in a country like the establishment of the commission, national plan, National Disaster Response Team.[8]It also specifies responsibilities and measures that government should take at the time of disaster under Chapter V.[9] Section 12 and 13 of the Act mentions minimum standard reliefs and loans repayment measures.[10]There are also NDMA Guidelines on each and every calamity. Regularly authority issues report and training materials to handle the disasters. The mechanism and policies are also issued by the authority. NDRF is a body that carries out rescue operations. In addition to infrastructure loss and relief measures the entire rehabilitation deeply affect the country in monetary terms.

ECONOMIC IMPACT

The economic impact of natural disasters such as cyclones, heavy rainfall and landslides is Multi-dimensional. Because in all cases there will be no direct economic impact on all the people. The unfortunate events cause an impact on different sections of society in varied forms either in a direct or indirect manner. In this section, the impact on the economy due to natural disasters is elucidated.

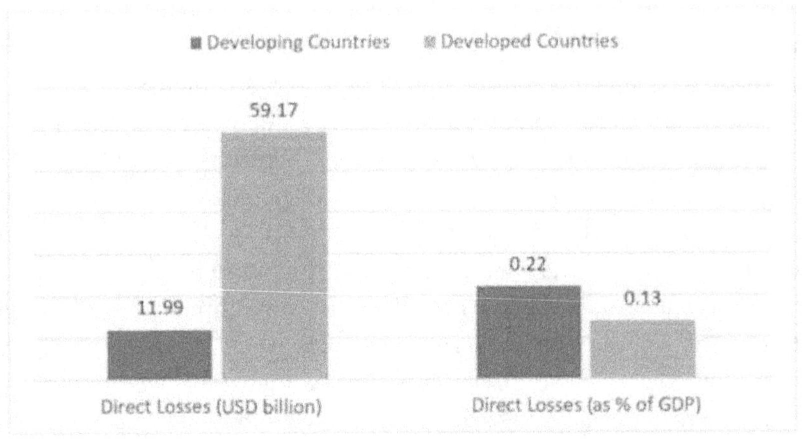

SHORT AND LONG - TERM IMPACTS

Another differentiation that can be made to understand the impact of disasters is in terms of long and short. Though some effects can be observed at the initial stages there are others that cause long term effects. Initially when disasters occur all economic activities will be disrupted for the short term depending on the intensity of the disaster. In this case, in short term it causes direct loss of human deaths, disabilities (labour), there will be loss of capital like damage to physical infrastructure, Assets and buildings. These effects subsequently result in low wages thereby reducing industrial/ agricultural outputs.[11]The GDP of the country will decrease due to the poor performance of the market. During cyclones in coastal states and heavy rains in smart cities, there will be a severe negative impact. The entire logistics business is disrupted along with stock markets decline. In comparison to developed countries, developing countries are sensitive to these economic slowdowns as coping up with the gap would be difficult for these countries. The economic impact ranges from short to medium term.

There are no proper studies conducted on estimates of long terms. However, natural disasters cause long term economic growth impacts as irregular human death disturbs the entire system. The human and physical capital severely affected that show long-term negatives. The funds utilized for rehabilitation, recovery measures, post-rehabilitation would have been utilized for social welfare which benefits the growth of the country.[12] This way, it eliminated future growth in the long term. The impact of landslides on the economy is the merger. But the human and capital loss exists even in this form of natural disaster. These can be mitigated easily by using a system of alarming and technological advancements.

All these are basic calculations made based on estimates by various centres and organizations. Firstly, the quantitative and theoretical assessments of economic impacts caused by natural disasters need to be made. It increases the reliability of data and takes necessary actions. Theoretical and computational macroeconomic models of natural disasters often lack spatial details; These models, like many empirical studies, ignore geography or operate on a large geographic scale, such as a region or country. Therefore, these approaches fail to take into account that most natural disasters initially have local effects; The location and the intensity of the disaster are important.

AGRICULTURE

Agriculture secures the livelihoods of more than 2.5 million people around the world. Given the sector's innate interactions with the environment, its direct dependence on natural resources for production and its importance for national socio-economic development, urgent and ambitious action is needed to build more resilient agricultural systems. The impact on agriculture caused due to natural disasters affect the food system.[13]

Agriculture lands are first affected due to cyclones and heavy rains. Recent Cyclone Amphan affected 13 million people and reduced agricultural productivity. This through the farmers and families dependent on crop into famine.[14] In the medium term with 2.13 percent effect on GDP growth they cause impact. Though water is important for agriculture, the excess amount washes away all the agricultural produce. These effects the productivity and supply chain however, it doesn't impact the economy at large.[15] In these instances, the schemes and loans, other rehabilitation plays a significant role. If not implemented properly large section of people suffer.

HOUSEHOLDS AND MSME'S

Smart cities like Hyderabad, Chennai and Mumbai face critical rainfall every year with increasing risks. The stress and effect in urban areas are vulnerable compared to rural areas. In the urban areas along with human loss, the economic loss is greater.[16] Natural Calamities impact severely the Rural areas and people already suffering from poverty increasing socio-economic vulnerability to the country. Great damage is caused due to cyclones, heavy rainfalls. The effect of these disasters can be observed in two-folds: Firstly, on the economy through impact on agriculture, businesses etc. and Second, well-being & welfare of people increasing state responsibility.[17] The end result of all these effects impact the Gross State Domestic Product (GSDP) of states[18] that in return alters the GDP of the nation.

Low-income and other marginalized groups are most exposed to the effects of climate change. Persistently high temperatures take a disproportionate toll on those who rely on manual labour outdoors or who live in crowded and poorly ventilated homes. Floods, storm surges, and hurricanes cause the greatest damage in low-income, densely populated communities that lack risk mitigation infrastructure. A study suggests that falling agricultural productivity and rising grain prices could increase India's national poverty rate by 3.5% by 2040 compared to the zero-warming scenario; this corresponds to around 50 million more poor people[19].

FINDINGS OF THE STUDY

From the research, it can be concluded that natural disasters are indispensable for any country including India that is geographically and environmentally vulnerable to these natural events. Every year an increase in these disasters can also be observed. At that stance, a direct relationship between economic growth and natural disasters can be drawn. Macroeconomy damage is more than the micro-economy. Despite this, the studies show that India is not prepared to face these disasters. In addition, negative local effects can be weakened or intensified by indirect positive or negative economic effects elsewhere. Another important observation from our review is that empirical models and approaches for assessing the economic impact of natural disasters have evolved as two independent branches of the literature and seem to have made little use of the results of both.

At large, the economic impacts can be divided into long and short terms. Depending on the disaster appropriate measures should be taken to mitigate the loss. For example: in landslides, the short -term loss can be observed such as human death, accidents, infrastructure and traffic. Warning Alert systems and awareness to people reduces the loss. Similarly, infrastructure should be built taking into consideration the disaster risks.

Despite policies such as disaster preparedness, resilience, risk reduction etc. on papers. Lack of proper infrastructure to mitigate damage, advanced technologies such as warning systems. State-level risk assessments are also essential to mitigate the loss. Though disasters are common in every other country the developing countries suffer severely due to lack of capacity. So, Mitigation is crucial rather should be a priority for India. Disaster Risk Reduction and investment in this mechanism are essential for sustainable development. For cyclones, the management of coastal zones is important. The states and coastal regions of Tamil Nadu, Andhra Pradesh, West Bengal, Odisha, Gujarat are prone to heavy floods. There is also an increase in these floods due to global warming and climate change.

Pro-active, resilience and preparedness are essential to sustain such economic shocks. Though there is legislation, guidelines, policies and directions many cases are being filed alleging lapses in the implementation mechanism. The institutional mechanism and policy implementation should be strong both in letter and spirit. Only then, the economic impact due to natural disasters can be mitigated or managed successfully.

CASE LAWS

Name of the Case: Swaraj Abhiyan v. Union of India[20]Citation: (2016) 7 SCC 498

The objective of the Case

In the present case, the court dealt with issues related to obligations of state governments in the implementation of enactments by Parliament such as the National Food Security Act, 2013 and the role of the Union is issuing directions to state on the implementation of parliament law.

Facts of the Case

Swaraj Abhiyan, the petitioner in the case filed a Public Interest Litigation (PIL) under Article 32 of the Constitution. In the year 2016, there are droughts in around 13 states such as Andhra Pradesh, Bihar, Uttar Pradesh and others. The petitioner alleges that despite the severe humanitarian crisis in regions due to droughts no proper relief and compensation was provided to the affected people. The organization prayed for compensation to affected farmers and subsidies and employment under MNREGA Scheme along with food grains under National Food Security Act, 2013. They also prayed for the implementation of Mid-day meal Schemes and crop loans for affected drought areas.

Issues Raised

1. What is the obligation of the Central government to ensure state governments and UT's implements laws passed by the parliament?
2. What happens when the Union doesn't issue necessary directions to States and UT's?

Plea of the Respondent

Several affidavits were filed by the Union of India and the State government. They submitted the appointment of officers & commissions were made and details regarding the implementation of the Act. Attorney General appeared on behalf of Union and state governments tried to convince the court regarding measures taken by governments.

Interpretation of the Court

The Supreme Court referred to the legal framework of the Disaster Management Act, 2005 elaborately and implementation mechanism carried out. The questions related to the declaration of droughts and mechanism under the National Food Security Act is interpreted as enshrined under the act and constitution. The indicative nature of manuals and guidelines was accepted. The court was directed to prepare Model rules under Section 15 of the National Food Security Act for the guidance of state governments.

Final Judgement

Among other things, instructions are given to states to establish an internal grievance mechanism and to appoint or appoint a district grievance officer as provided for in the 2013 law; form the State Food Commission to oversee and review the implementation of the 2013 law; in states where drought has been declared or may be declared in the future, all households must receive monthly food grain entitlement under the 2013 law. It also instructed the Government of India to ensure that workers whose wages have been more than 15 days behind receive compensation for late payments under the 2005 Act; The Government of India is instructed to ensure the establishment of the Central Employment Guarantee Council under the 2005 Act. Petition kept pending to further issue directions in future.

Referred Cases

1. People's Union for Civil liberties v. Union of India, (2013) 2 SCC 688.
2. Essar Steel Limited v. Union of India, 2016 (4) SC 242.

Name of the Case: Gaurav Kumar Bansal v. Union of India[21]

Citation: (2017) 6 SCC 730

Objective of the case

In the case, the court dealt with Uttarakhand floods and landslides that took place in the year 2013. Petitioners questioned the actions and preparedness of state disaster management authority in the mitigation of disaster. The court dealt with the role of the state in disaster management.

Facts of the Case

A petition is filed under Article 32 of the Constitution on the Uttarakhand disaster. Petitioner alleges that lack of proper implementation of Disaster Management Act, 2005 and preparedness lead to adverse impact, loss, life in the cyclone, landslides. They allege that the state is responsible for the loss and seek directions to be issued by courts for implementation of the Act.

Issues Raised

1. Whether the formation of an Advisory Committee is mandatory under Disaster Management Act, 2005?
2. What is the responsibility and role of the state under the Disaster Management Act?

Plea of the Respondent

The State Government filed affidavits stating actions taken by the government. In response, the central government also immediately took action after filing the case. It issued directions to Chief Secretaries of Disaster Management Authorities to frame standards that need to be taken for victims of the disaster.

Interpretation of the Court

The Supreme Court revisited all key provisions of Act i.e. Section 11, 23, 31, 7,8, 12 and 14. The provisions related to the formulation of the National Plan include a state-specific plan for disaster management. It found that in the past 10 years there has been no state plan formulated. It considered the actions taken after 2017 as the formation of an advisory committee by state governments.

Final Judgment

The court held that the establishment of an Advisory Committee is not mandatory. The State Disaster Management Authority has the discretion to form the committee as per requirement and necessity. It further declared that the state followed all necessary steps and no directions are required. However, it stated that state and National & State Disaster management should be vigilant, prepared for disasters. Hence, disposed of the petition.

<u>CONCLUSION</u>

Economic loss and disasters are interrelated aspects. However, the impact can be reduced with due efforts and mechanisms. India is one of the developing countries fighting against the evils of poverty since independence. The effects of disaster further worsen the situation. As observed above, some million loss occurs and continues to take place due to disasters that affect the economic growth of the country. However, with proper infrastructure, mechanisms and Disaster resilience economic impacts of disasters can be controlled. Climate change alert and its adverse impacts are being studied and evaluated. It is a caution towards declining economic growth. Proper assessments and an action plan are essential to reduce economic costs. The study is an effort to elucidate the relationship between economic growth and natural disasters.

CHAPTER TWENTY-EIGHT

SHOULD JUVENILES BE TRIED AND TREATED AS ADULTS?

Author: Deivanayagi H, V year of B.B.A.,LL.B.(Hons.) from Tamilnadu Dr Ambedkar Law University, Chennai

INTRODUCTION

JUVENILES, the word itself meant that childish or immature person. It represents the young person who is not yet old enough to be considered as an adult. In India children of different ages are considered to be a juvenile delinquent. However, the question is whether the age factor alone determines the criminal requirements? Recent survey says that crimes where juveniles involved are dacoit, gang rape and murder etc. Experts suggest that our Indian law couldn't able to cope with the current scenario.it should have some changes that the juveniles should be treated as an adult in severe crimes. This article will discuss in detail about the reasons behind that.

JUVENILE DELIQUENT

Juvenile delinquency is one of the most crucial and controversial issue that have to look upon. A recent development in the environment has changed the mind state of children of this age physically as well as mentally. They are having a quick learning capacity which may lead them to go to the next end. The development in the field of science can bring the whole world into our hands. Children under the age of 18 are easily exploited by them, which is one of the major causes to emerge him as a delinquent. Most of the teenagers are driven to some crimes due to the family background, mental conflicts, friend and companions etc.no one is a born criminal, some circumstances are shaped them to involve in these kinds of illegal activities.

Nowadays, social media also played a vital role, which will ruin the brains of the youngsters.

As we discussed earlier, our Indian law having certain branches for juvenile crimes which are not that much effective for some exceptional juveniles who are all involved in certain heinous crimes. They should bring some changes on that. There are always certain pros and cons regarding this issue, should we try the juveniles as adults? At the outset it is believed that a child is a fragile, both physically and mentally. For such reasons they created separated category for them.in the case of Rooper v. Simmons[i] the court held that the reason behind the differentiation between the juveniles and adults were the level of maturity, surrounding influences and the high possibility to reform.

Subsequently, if juveniles are treated as adults, they will have their sentence along with the adults.in such cases; there is high possibility of choosing the adult offenders as their idols. They will be easily exploited and also chances are there for physical assault to take place[ii]. At the other hand, let us discuss the below cases. On December 16th, 2012, a girl was raped and killed on a moving bus by a group of 5 people including a 17-year-old minor in Delhi[iii]. On November 2013, a jeweler's wife was killed by a group of five juveniles, who escaped from a juvenile home, and they were also eloped for taking 10 lakh cash and 50 kg of silver jewelry[iv]. On December 24, 2015, three juveniles were convicted for killing a police officer at the court complex, at karkardooma. These are all some of the cases which involved some exceptional juveniles which I mentioned earlier.

Further, people doing such illegal activities making use of these juvenile crimes as a defence. Instead of involving themselves in the crimes, they are using these people who have not attained majority[v]. The lesser punishment is one of the major cause for this. For example, section 302 of IPC prescribes the punishment for murder for an adult. It says any person who commits murder shall be punishable with death or imprisonment for life and also be liable to fine. At the same time earlier when a juvenile commits a murder, they are free from the criminal liability under the section 82 and 83 of Indian penal code, as they are not capable of doing such crimes.

Subsequently, our parliament enacted a new statue exclusively for the children between the age of 16 to 18. It says that children between the age of 16 to 18 can be considered as an adult for heinous or terrible crimes. For them the punishment will be imprisonment of maximum three years under the juvenile justice (care and protection) Act, 2015.it is no way possible that children under the age of 18 can never be punished for a crime. Why does the age factor alone stands to classify them is a big question mark till date?

In the case of State of Maharashtra vs. Vijay Mohan Jadhav&Ors (2021)[vi], a primary accused of the horrible rape was sentenced with three years of imprisonment under the juvenile justice act where the others were punished with death sentence.subsequently; in any cases the word heinous should be highlighted. Section 2(33) of the juvenile justice act 2015 provides that offenses for which the punishment under the Indian penal code or any other legislations is seven years or more, then it will be considered as a heinous crime. However, the same was demonstrated by Bombay High Court in another case[vii].

<u>Reasons why juveniles should be considered as an adult?</u>

- It will reduce the chance of repeating the crime for multiple time:

A recent survey says that in 2018 the number of crimes committed by a juvenile is 21, it became 28 in 2019 and 36 in 2020.it also says that in the survey 59 juveniles were committing the same offense in the previous year's 36 crimes. The present law couldn't able to cope up with that to reduce such rates. By trying them as an adult we can prevent them from becoming a habitual offender.

- It treats the juveniles who are almost adult as a part of adult system to ensure justice

The major reason behind this is to prevent the homicide offense. A recent study in U.S. provides that in 2016 among the homicide offenders 9% of offenders were juveniles. Within that 79% were the one who are between the ages of 16-18. By treating them as adults will teach the accountability for the crime.

- Serious actions for severe heinous crimes that they deserve

The present law is so lenient for the juveniles which may lead them to do severe terrible offences. Some people using the juveniles as the key way to do certain offence. To prevent all these, there should be some changes which will teach them the seriousness of the offence. Any actions should take neither based on the age nor on the law.it should be based on the seriousness of the crime and the consequences and also the level of maturity[viii].

- Bring justice to the victims

The action will correct the blind justice and bring justice to the victims. And it will also prevent the youth from losing their entire life. It's quite sensible to filter out the juveniles based of level of maturity and consequences, the future of this will be bigger than what we expected[ix].

<u>Conclusion</u>

Therefore, based on the above discussion, we can make a conclusion that the answer to the question will be neither yes nor no.it should be completely based on the cases and the circumstances of that.it will vary for every case.my personal opinion is that the juvenile justice system should not consider every juvenile at the same level of maturity. It should not classify them only bases on their age alone.it should focus on the nature of crime instead of the offender. And also we can't blindly believe that juveniles who are all about to become as adults should treat as adult.it will vary from juvenile to juvenile. In addition to their age, their level of maturity, personal life, education, physical capability also should be considered to determine any case. No one is a born criminal, circumstances may lead them to do. By making our justice system more effective today, will definitely bring a better tomorrow.

CHAPTER TWENTY-NINE

SOCIAL MEDIA AND RACISM

Author: Kaulik Mitra, II year of B.A.,LL.B. from KIIT School of Law

Abstract

In today's day and age everyone is using social media. In fact, there are now so many types of social media platforms, all having diverse and varied functions or programs. This means that social media has almost become an extension of real life. Whatever exists in real life, exists on social media these days. Naturally, this translates to the negatives of human nature as much as it does to the positives. Racism is one such evil that has made this unfortunate transition. Here, we look at racism on social media, what the different platforms have done or are doing about it, the current provisions in place, and what can be done about it.

Keywords- Social media, racism

Introduction

The recent Euro 2020 final and the subsequent reactions to England's loss brought a lot of attention to the problem of racism on social media. The fact is that it has existed for a long time now and unfortunately as well, it is scarily common. Going back to the England incident, what happened was that in the penalty shootout Jadon Sancho, Marcus Rashford and Bukayo Saka all missed, handing the cup over to Italy. Now such failures lead to criticism, which is harsh, for such is the nature of sport that one team has to lose, but also to some extent fair. But it is only fair when its limited to the failure. The sad part is that some people only seemed to notice that fact that all of three of these players were 'of colour' so as to speak. Regardless to say but of course the colour of one's skin has no relation with their actions or in this case mistakes. All three of these players are fine young men and exceptional footballers, the type people should celebrate and cherish and not racially abuse. However within seconds of the match ending, they received unbelievable amount of racial hatred. Their comments and inboxes were full of derogatory racial abuses and emojis of similiar negative connotations.

The matter of fact is that this is not an isolated incidence. It is unnervingly regular and repeatedly keeps happening at levels subliminal to the public conscience. The thing is, racially abusing someone shouldn't be as easy as it seems to be. Racism is ultimately an extremely grave and serious problem, the history and even present repercussions of which are widely known to everyone. Ultimately it is easy to say that racism on social media wouldn't be taking place if the root of the evil is dealt with; racism itself. However that is easier said than done because the evil is so deeply entrenched within the fabric of some individuals, families or even communities.

Existing social media policies for racism

Social media platforms of course have their own rules and regulations pertaining to racism. This can most commonly be seen under the umbrella of hate speech. The most popular social media companies often own more than one platform. Facebook for example owns others like Instagram and Whatsapp but still their guidelines are different because of differences in the platforms. Here's what Facebook have as a part of their community guidelines against hate speech - "we define hate speech as a direct attack on people - based on what we call protected traits: race, ethnic identity, national origin, disability, religious identity, caste, sexual identity, sexuality, gender identity and serious disease. We interpret attacks as violent or inhumane speech, harmful stereotypes, derogatory statements, expressions of contempt, hatred or exclusion, cursing, and calls for exclusion or segregation. We also prohibit harmful stereotypes that have historically been used to attack, intimidate, or exclude certain groups. We define content as inhumane comparisons that are often associated with offline violence." They also mention a list of actions that users can't do in respect to these restrictions. Violent speech or support in the form of written or visual descriptions is prohibited as is inhumane speech or description by comparing, generalizing or presenting inappropriate behavioral statements be it in written or visual form.[1]

Twitter say a similar thing as well, not allowing anything thatpromotes violence against or directly attacks or threatens other people on the basis of race, ethnicity, national origin, caste, sexual orientation, gender, gender identity, religious affiliation, age, disability, or serious disease. According to their policy, they also do not allow accounts whose primary purpose is inciting harm towards others on the basis of these categories. An interesting difference between the two sites however is the fact that Facebook's definition of hate speech is broad, and covers "violent or dehumanising speech, harmful stereotypes, statements of inferiority, expressions of contempt, disgust or dismissal, cursing and calls for exclusion or segregation."

Twitter, however, takes a narrower view, and bans only hate speech that could "promote violence against or directly attack or threaten other people on the basis of race" or other protected characteristics. Users can be penalised for "targeting individuals with repeated slurs, tropes or other content that intends to dehumanise, degrade or reinforce negative or harmful stereotypes about a protected category".[2]

Instagram are a photo/ video sharing platform who are also owned by Facebook. They have around 1.074 billion monthly users. Instagram's policy seems a little more broader. Their website says "Our rules against hate speech don't tolerate attacks on people based on their protected characteristics, including race or religion. We strengthened these rules last year, banning more implicit forms of hate speech, like content depicting Blackface and common antisemitic tropes. We take action whenever we become aware of hate speech, and we're continuously improving our detection tools so we can find it faster". They also recognise that a lot of the abuse actually takes place in private inboxes or Direct Messages as they call them. " Between July and September of last year, we took action on 6.5 million pieces of hate speech on Instagram, including in DMs, 95% of which we found before anyone reported it" - Instagram add. They are also working with law enforcement especially in the UK and will be assisting them with information in cases whenever asked for. Moreover, they won't be allowing racist messages to be sent, prohibiting the person from sending any messages at all for a set time period. Repeat offenders can have their accounts disabled. They also say that they willdisable new accounts created to get around their messaging restrictions, and will continue to disable accounts they find that are created purely to send abusive messages.[3]

The video platform Youtube who are owned by Google are also quite strict about preventing racism. Their policies say clearly that hate speech is not allowed on YouTube. They also say that they remove content promoting violence or hatred against individuals or groups. They specify a long list of things that are rightly prohibited in videos on their platform. On violation of these regulations, punishment ranges from removal of content, demonetisation, temporary ban to even permanent deletion of channel.[4]

<u>Discussion</u>

What can be improved?

Although these are the existing provisions to act against racism in the most popular social media platforms, it is important to note that racism on these social media platforms are still commonly prevalent and even widespread. There's no doubt that further and constant improvements need to be made in this field. The world's largest social networks say that racism is not welcome on their platforms, but the combination of weak law enforcement and weak rules has made hate prevalent. Another significant problem that arises is the existence of automated moderators rather than actual human beings acting as moderators. A number of well wishing users were surprised by this when they tried to report racist content. "Because we receive a large number of reports, our review team is unable to review your report," many users get told "However, our technology found that this article cannot violate our community guidelines." Instead, they are advised to personally block users who posted abusive content or silence the phrases so they couldn't see them. These posts are undeniably racist, but there is no obvious way to attract actual human attention and force the issue on them. There have been calls for the social media companies to use their expertise in artificial intelligence to detect racist messages, as and when they are being written, and urge users to think twice or avoid publishing them.[5]

But another idea that seems to be increasingly popular is to end anonymity on social media so that racists can be tracked. However this is not a solution. This can, instead of solving one problem aggravate another. If social media companies and governments force users to reveal their legal identities, it will cause serious harm, especially to those who are already at risk, such as people of color, women, and LGBTQ+ community members. For many people who have long been excluded from physical and cyberspace, or who have been marginalized and attacked, anonymity is a survival tool. For these people, an anonymous account is the only option to interact with the media, express themselves and share information online in a relatively secure way. Similarly, survivors of domestic violence have found a safe place online, thanks to their ability to stay in touch and communicate while maintaining their identity.[6]Numerous studies and testimonials have shown that for millions of people, anonymity online is essential for personal safety and existence of freedom.The best we can do as responsible digital citizens is first of all to report racist content and also make sure that we do not unintentionally spread or amplify it.[7]

<u>Conclusion</u>

Racism on social media is an extension of racist tendencies in real life. Hence the punishment must also be an extension from social media to real life. What this means is that even apart from the punishments that have been mentioned above that are dished out by the social media platforms, penalizing offenders by the book of the law is also a need of the times. Therefore it is important for law enforcement to take these cases that occur on social media as seriously as the ones that do take place in real life. The UK law enforcement have particular provisions to take action against racism. In the United Kingdom, although you may find a lot of offensive material on the Internet, only a small part is illegal.[8] When the crime defined by the law is committed out of hate motives, online hate materials will be registered as a hate crime by the police. When online materials are motivated by hatred but do not reach the threshold of crime, they are recorded as hate incidents. Law enforcement agencieslike the police have the responsibility to promote good relationships between different parts of our communities, but they do not have powers to control offensive thoughts or words unless they are shared illegally.The Director of Public Prosecutions, who has the responsibility for deciding who should be prosecuted has produced guidance to prosecutors to ensure consistency. That is the situation in UK.[9]

In India, the legislation isn't as well constructed or developed. "The Government of India in its affidavit dated 8 July 2015 before the Delhi High Court as well in written replies in the Rajya Sabha on 18 March 2015 and 26 July 2017 assured that the MHA was in the process of finalising a comprehensive bill for insertion of new sections of 153C and 509A in Indian Penal Code (IPC) to address racial attacks especially on the people from North-Eastern States." IPC Section 153(A) and 295(A) speaks about the restrictions to freedom of expression and this does include statements that promote hatred on the grounds of race. Australia and Germany have some of the strictest laws and regulations on social media, imposing fines and imprisonment for "inaction against extremist hate speech" in a short period of time.[10]

At the same time, the EU has also formulated a code of conduct to ensure that hate speech does not spread. Most other countries have been struggling between threats to technology companies and platforms and law enforcement responses to non-anonymous users, but given the transnational nature of the technology, consistent global regulatory standards will have to ensure the unity of governance and supervision, and at the same time maintain specificity as well as consider local conditions. With the emergence of new platforms such as TikTok, online media and social responsibility are constantly evolving. This makes it all the harder. Things like these have lead to people in charge of the social media platforms saying that it is virtually impossible to completely weed out racism from their websites.Both Facebook CEO Mark Zuckerberg and Instagram head Adam Mosseri publicly admitted that their platforms will never be fully rid of harmful content.[11] Ultimately the thing is no matter how much social media platforms improve their systems, the only way to completely eliminate racism is through education of the masses.

CHAPTER THIRTY

EXPECTATIONS VS EDUCATION

Author: Anjali Tiwari, LLM(CORPORATE COMMERICAL LAW)

"Every child wants to be the star of there parents"

The society, in which we are living only want their child to be excellent without knowing what their child want to do and how they are feeling like they want to be a part of this race or not. Expectation is something that is creating a gap between the bond of parents and their child. Today, each and every parent is letting their child to be in the race of competition irrespective of their want and ability. The pressure which is on the generation to be the best and to fulfill the expectations of their parents is letting them towards anxiety and depression.

This situation is further aggravated by the education system by imposing much more academic pressure for showing there excellence without measuring the capacity and ability. The education system mostly focuses on the performance of student in exam irrespective of fact that the student is getting concept or just acting as a rattutota.

PARENTAL PRESSURE

Every parent want their child to be the best and to stand in the society for which somewhere they are suppressing the talent of their child to make them focus on their academics. The comparison with the other child is somewhere demotivating their own child and making them to think that they are not able to fulfill the expectations of their parents, this is also the reason of unemployment as 70% of the generation is working in the direction in which they have least interest and they are on that path only for their parents to be a star in there parents eyes. Every parent want their child to be better thansharmajika beta. Many of the students who are in a particular field even don't know why they are studying that subject and what they want to do in that field. Passions like writing, photography, sketching, dancing, etc. are just hobby and can't be an employment as these are not acceptable as a profession in the society, some parents want to support their children but then they also think that chaar log kyakahenge, which make them to get back there support. In the race of expectation, parents are not able to understand that what their children want to do and to be. The 'generation gap' and 'what others will think', these things are creating barrier in between the parents and their children.

<u>ACADEMIC PRESSURE</u>

Institutions want to make toppers irrespective of the fact that the students are really able to do all that work or are they really getting concepts or just learning them to make a good score. In school, teachers mainly focus on the textbook rather than the practical knowledge and only expect to memorize the concepts and after that the other pressure to do other works after school time, for more enhancement of knowledge, after school, maximum students go to tuition's. In between all this, the school forgets that the student should get time to focus on other activities also and also focus on mental as well as physical health. They have to focus to get better college for further education which is a type of pressure on them in that small age.

In colleges, the students have to attend a long tiring sessions and after that they have to make assignments, presentations, other works which are assigned to them, they are not getting time to be mentally fit. Most of the students of this age are found depressed due to the pressure of good performance and career. In this way the pressure continues from the time of school to institution and led students to go on such path of anxiety and depression.

<u>WHAT CAN BE DONE</u>

To curb this situation, everyone have to play some role, both teachers and parents.

Parents can do

- Parents can ask their children that what they want to do in life, can discuss about their career.
- If the child is having some pressure and anxiety then parents should have a word with them that whatever will happen, they are with them.
- Parents have to accept the fact that every child is different in its own way and should not compare their child with others.

- Parents should focus on the positive things and must appreciate them on even there small success which will build confidence in them.
- Parents should think about the impression of their words on their children before uttering them, sometimes some words let the child feel that they are not capable of doing that specific thing and needs some appreciation from their parents.
- Parents have to place the profession and there happiness above the society, society is not going to take care of that child and going to give them bread and butter.
- Parents should discuss the future plans of their child like what they want to do, how they want to do, they will be able to feed themselves and their family by what they are planning to do.
- Parents should tell the pros and cons of everything, they should never impose their dreams but always maintain a balance between the dreams of their children and of them.

Teachers can do

- Teachers should focus more on practical knowledge of student than theoretical knowledge.
- Teachers should acknowledge the efforts of students in that particular work and always encourage them to do much better.
- Teacher should make the environment of class as such that the student should feel free to express their views.
- Teachers should educate their students about time management, how to make a balance between their educational and social life.
- Teachers should give assignments and projects alternatively so as to reduce the burden of student and letting them to have some time for other activities also.
- Teachers should teach students to write qualitative work and not quantitative work, they should teach the importance of giving quality content.
- Teachers should concentrate on the deeper understanding of student rather than only giving notes to them of that specific topic.

FINAL WORDS

In this decade of stress, anxiety and depression which are leading them to suicides and other harmful activities, parents, teachers and other closed once should observe the activities and changes in their child/student and must have a word with them, maybe that child want to express something. It's needed to reduce the parental as well as academic pressure on that child. Its needed to appreciate the child when they are doing something good rather than comparing their success with other. We must observe the obstacles that students are having in their path of success and if we are not able to solve them then must at least wave its back for solving that on their own. We must appreciate its profession what they are planning to do irrespective of position and package, happiness and dedication of child matters the most. Every child is unique in their own way with some special talent and we must appreciate that talent at every point.